MANAGING THE DEMAND–SUPPLY CHAIN

Wiley Operations Management Series for Professionals

MANAGING THE DEMAND–SUPPLY CHAIN

VALUE INNOVATIONS FOR CUSTOMER SATISFACTION

WILLIAM E. HOOVER JR.
EERO ELORANTA
JAN HOLMSTRÖM
KATI HUTTUNEN

JOHN WILEY & SONS, INC.

New York • Chichester • Weinheim • Brisbane • Singapore • Toronto

Published by John Wiley & Sons, Inc.
Published simultaneously in Canada.

Library of Congress Cataloging-in-Publication Data:

Managing the demand-supply chain : value innovations for customer satisfaction / Eero Eloranta [et al.]
    p. cm. — (Wiley operations management series for professionals)
  Includes bibliographical references and index.
  ISBN 0-471-38499-2 (cloth : alk. paper)
  1. Business logistics. 2. Distribution of goods—Management. 3. Industrial procurement—Management. I. Eloranta, Eero, 1950– II. Series.

HD38.5.M363 2001
658.7′2—dc21   00-043696

Printed in the United States of America.

10 9 8 7 6 5 4 3 2

Preface

TEAM

In late 1998, a representative from Wiley visited one of the Stanford Global Supply Chain Forum events where Kati Huttunen was making a presentation and suggested afterward that Kati should write a book on the novel idea of Demand Chain Management. At that time, Kati was extremely busy with assignments with Nokia Mobile Phones and she hesitated to initiate the demanding effort of writing a manuscript for the global professional community in the field.

However, when Kati mentioned the idea to Professor Eero Eloranta, her former boss at Helsinki University of Technology (HUT) and Nokia, he was enthusiastic about the challenge. Back at HUT, after his prolonged sabbatical with Nokia, Eero felt a professional obligation to share with peers what Nokia had achieved in demand and supply chain management. However, the potential bias toward the telecommunications industry needed to be addressed. They did not want to publish a case study that applied only to a fast-changing industry. They wanted a wider perspective. The solution was closer than expected: Jan Holmström, with a doctorate in industrial engineering and management, had recently returned to HUT and had a track record including automotive industries, daily consumables, and pulp and paper. Jan had worked for Unilever in the area of logistics and IT applications and he was an expert on ERP applications. Jan was the first of us who realized and accepted the magnitude of the book writing task.

After leaving Unilever, Jan joined McKinsey, where among other things, Jan worked for Bill Hoover's supply chain management team. In the early 1990s, Bill and others evolved the revolutionary concept of Microcosms—a customer-oriented, outside-in, order-to-payment process development and implementation method. This methodology had been widely used for the benefit of different industries.

Bill's customer centric ideas contrasted with the mainstream business process reengineering recipes, overloaded with IT jargon and internal focus. But Bill was after more: A group of experts around Bill and Jan from McKinsey seconded by Eero, set up a taskforce to create a new theory in the field. But it was not enough, with a mere supply focus, the service needs of the customers would never be identified and so never fulfilled. A demand chain was to be incorporated in the core of the theory, and the idea of the Value Offering Point (VOP) emerged.

After pondering for some weeks, we agreed as a team of four to write the manuscript: Kati represented innovativeness and deep understanding of fast-changing industries, in particular telecommunications; Eero stood for structural consistency and integrity; Jan was the writing machine responsible for more than half of the text; and Bill was a living case bank encyclopedia and practitioner and the key editor of all the texts.

THEME

Customer-centric integrated end-to-end demand and supply chains turned out to be the theme of our book: How to create service value innovations for the customer and how to create customer lock-in? Is there something more advantageous than the build-to-order collaborative models? Where and how to offer value to the customers? How to minimize forecasting error-prone activities by optimizing the location of order penetration points? These fundamental questions are raised—and answered—in the subsequent pages of our book.

Several leading edge companies in the field have inspired us, including Dell, Cisco, and Nokia. Dell is a landmark for the "box-business" community. Cisco is the company that set the rules for the systems companies in the Internet era. Nokia is one of the leading companies in mass-scale operations, sourcing, and distribution.

Our book presents some basic innovations that will outlast the e-business hype. Nevertheless, e-business was a major catalyst and was imperative to create quantum leaps in the customer value innovations. We offer some insights into what we think will be the next major—still largely uncovered—source for value innovations: Wireless communication and mobile Internet will make it possible to reach anyone and anything, anytime, anywhere, and has the potential to revolutionize demand-supply chain management again.

WILLIAM E. HOOVER, JR.
EERO ELORANTA
JAN HOLMSTRÖM
KATI HUTTUNEN

Acknowledgments

We feel deeply indebted to a large cadre of academics and professionals in the field. We would like to mention a few of the people who have most impacted the birth of this book.

Pertti Korhonen, senior vice president of Nokia Mobile Phones, changed the performance of Nokia global logistics from the "average" company to the level of "competitive excellence." Pertti started with a lean team, changed the way one segment was served and then scaled up and turned the inventories into profits. Without this, we should have practically nothing new to tell to the global business community.

Tom Vollmann from IMD is the foresighted authority in the field who has been a tireless crusader toward the deeper understanding of the complex phenomena in the industrial life. Tom has been, for decades, an incredible reservoir of revolutionary ideas toward better solutions to the industrial challenges. Tom also has provided us valuable feedback on the ideas presented in the book.

Hau Lee from Stanford University has been an inspiration for some of the ideas presented. He created the collaborative Stanford University SCM Forum, where the authors and the publisher met.

Jukka Ranta from Aspocomp has experimented with the methodology presented here. His personal inventions on supply chain dynamics and the associated impact of the build-in inertia will impact many major corporations in the coming years.

Joachim Westh started the McKinsey supply chain thinking that led to Microcosms in the early 1990s. As a skilled practitioner, Joachim experimented with the idea of transparent end-to-end chains led by cross-functional team. He and Bengt Starke led many of the early studies, where the basic methodology was born.

Antti Vasara, formerly of McKinsey, now working for Sonera, and Perttu Louhiluoto of McKinsey, have been extremely helpful to the authors by providing a sounding board for many new ideas, including the original VOP-thinking.

Many of the professionals within Nokia have contributed to our work, including Per Högberg, Tapio Järvenpää, Mikko Kosonen, Marko Luhtala, Hille Ranta-aho, Taina Riihimäki, Juha Usva and Eero Virros—all professionals who have expanded our understanding about the huge hidden potential of customer centric development, regarding both traditional business models and the future e-business enabled advanced models.

Panu Kaila from Elcoteq has been a co-creator of many application-oriented ideas. Panu positively challenged any experimental ideas.

Jussi Heikkilä, formerly from IMD and currently at HUT, has provided us extensive insight from systems business. Jussi's research and eduction work with various global corporations ranging from construction to software has subjected our thinking to tests that have forced us to polish our ideas.

Unfortunately we haven't space to list all of our other friends and peers at Nokia, McKinsey, and HUT who have materially contributed to our book. We sincerely thank you all.

Finally, we are members of four loving families. Without their love and support, this writing would have no purpose.

W.E.H.
E.E.
J.H.
K.H.

Contents

Chapter 1

Introduction

This book is about demand-supply chain management—which is both about doing business with the customer in a completely different way (value innovation) and about leveraging change at the customer end so you can do what you now do, only better (process improvement).

■ SERVING THE CUSTOMER—INNOVATION OR PROCESS IMPROVEMENT?

How do you fulfill customer demand in the best possible way? Is it innovation and applications, or operational excellence and responsiveness?

The answer is both: Process efficiency and innovation need to evolve together. To succeed, you must operate more effectively and innovate the business concurrently. And, you need to do it across the entire demand-supply chain.

How can you do this? Having competitive products and the right supply chain for the average customer is not enough. Your supply chain has to be right for the individual customer as well. The demand chain—the chain of activities that communicates demand from markets to suppliers—offers suppliers a wide range of opportunities to differentiate their value offering. It is your customer relationship, plus your operation and the customer's operation, that makes up a demand-supply chain. It is in the demand-supply chain that you need to start a coevolutionary process. The customer must leverage suppliers to improve their performance (outsourcing), while suppliers coopt customer competencies (collaborative business) to innovate their business model.

How can you navigate more safely in a changing business environment, and begin this coevolutionary advance toward business excellence? A new concept to describe the customer relationship is needed to take the next step in supply chain management, that is, to create demand-supply chains that do things differently and more efficiently at the same time. We have coined a new term—VOP[1]—for "Value Offering Point" to describe how the supply chain is linked to customer demand. The VOP is the companion on the customer side for the better known OPP, "Order Penetration Point," on the supplier side that has brought us "build-to-order" and "assemble-to-order."

The VOP defines how and when a customer makes the purchase decision. For example, a grocery supply chain that ends on a supermarket shelf dictates that the consumer's purchase decision is made in the supermarket, in front of a shelf full of competing items. A grocery supply chain that ends with home delivery, however, can make a much wider range of offers to the consumer, not only offers of different products, but of different services. The same standard shopping basket can be delivered automatically to the consumer every week, or the vendor can come and check the consumers' refrigerator to stock up on what has run out or gone stale. By moving the VOP, we can change an "order fulfillment" business model to a number of powerful "order-less fulfillment" models. First, we can provide the consumer with a "Don't Run Out" replenishment service and then, taking it one step further, go into a "Supply-to-Menu" service when all missing ingredients are automatically delivered to fulfill the customer's plan.

Now that e-business applications are becoming more powerful by the day, understanding the VOP is critical for companies that want to improve both efficiency and customer value. The VOP is a new, powerful concept that helps you focus on where and how to use new technology solutions for maximum customer value. Additionally, choosing the VOP with care can also give the supplier company more degrees of freedom to change operations internally, for example, by using earlier information on demand for optimizing production and distribution.

■ E-BUSINESS AND THE DEMAND-SUPPLY CHAIN

How does a company's demand-supply chain change with new available e-business technology? There are two basic ways this can happen: The company can do what it did before, but on a larger scale and faster; or, the company can use the new technology to innovate the way it does business.

The first way to change with new technology—to do what the company did before, only on a much larger scale—is obviously the most common. Historically, new technology has often been used to break away from scale constraints. Precision machine tools gave us mass production, broadcast media created mass marketing, and information technology has enabled producers to mass-customize their product designs for individual consumers and business customers. A company can also speed up its existing processes. Solectron, a company that provides electronics manufacturing services to leading original equipment manufacturers reduced its own procurement cycle from one month to one day with electronic commerce.

The other option is to use new technology to innovate your business—to offer the customer something more than a product or a service. After establishing itself on the Web in 1996, Grainger has come up with a winning new business formula. Instead of offering commodity products, the company offers a service to its customers. The company offers business customers "one site–one order–one answer" for office, production, and maintenance supplies. A customer company that makes all its purchases through the site outsources supplier management and vendor selection processes to Grainger, and simplifies its own internal material handling and accounts payable. The differences between offering a commodity product or a service and a value-added service are subtle, but the key is whether a relationship is created, maintained, and developed.

New technology can and should be used by companies both to improve scale economics and to create more valuable relationships. But what is the marching order? Is it innovation before scale and real-time operations, or building up technological capabilities to operate effectively before innovating the business relationships?

Innovating the business relationship without developing the capabilities to deliver will obviously not work, as so many e-tail start-ups have painfully discovered.

But going the other way—imagining that innovation follows automatically from technological capability—is equally risky. The risk is that electronic business will make you a supplier to online commodity exchanges and reverse markets allowing the customer to cherry-pick your offering. At the same time, your suppliers may be locking you firmly into their supply chain integration webs and networks. As a result, your company runs the risk of becoming a faster and more efficient, but lower margin, commodity supplier.

The solution is to do both—evolve process efficiency and innovation together. This is what demand-supply chain management is essentially about, and it is the topic of this book.

■ DEMAND-SUPPLY CHAIN MANAGEMENT IN PRACTICE

What does demand-supply chain management mean in practice: What do you do to innovate and improve process efficiency at the same time? This book answers that question, while keeping in mind the issues facing a supplier of physical goods in both an e-business and m-business environment.

Chapter 2 explains how to go beyond the customer order to the customer's demand chain. This approach allows you to see new business opportunities based on understanding the customer's business purpose, planning process, and consumption of your product. This is what demand-supply chain management is about. It is a new way of combining classic marketing and supply chain management operationally.

Chapter 3 focuses on how demand-supply chains work. The basic challenge is to make offers to improve your customer's operation, and use that change to improve your own. This coevolutionary process has produced such winning value configurations as IKEA, Wintel, Carrefour, and Dell to name a few.

In Chapter 4, you acquire the basic tools to reconfigure your demand-supply chains. You learn how to systematically look for opportunities to improve the value you offer your customer (VOP), while leveraging the customer relationship for improved efficiency. That is, how to define win-win configurations. Chapter 5 provides examples of these techniques.

Chapter 6 shows you how to put the demand-supply chain to use in developing not only your customer relationships, but also your own supplier relationships.

Chapter 7 is dedicated to the challenges of implementation when many companies and organizations are involved. Topics include setting up microcosms to speed up innovation and piloting, and using the logic of coevolution—sell-in where there is buy-in—to successfully implement collaborative solutions.

The challenge of managing information technology (IT) for business value in the demand-supply chain is covered in Chapter 8. The challenge is to stretch the business to its full potential. The full potential has only been reached when the latest IT is no more the enabler for future improvements, but already the constraint in current operations. We use examples to describe the challenges today.

Chapter 9 shows how to make value-driven IT a tool for quickly exploiting new business opportunities. The IT value capture method consists of identifying opportunity, setting the scope, innovating the business solution, and making the resource and partnering decisions. The value capture method then drives development of the IT supply chain, including strategy and concept initiatives, piloting and industrializing solutions, implementation, and business use. It can often lead to stunning 80/20 solutions (80 percent of the benefit, with 20 percent of the effort), where previously 100/100 solutions were abandoned as impossible, or took years to implement.

Finally, in Chapter 10, the discussion turns to how the next wave of breakthrough technology, wireless communication and mobile commerce applications, will further change the supply chain. Wireless applications will start to wipe out the boundaries between the virtual and real world. For the supply chain, this means being able to link the physical flow of goods directly into information systems. Or in other words, databases and record keeping can start being replaced by wireless tracking. For the demand chain, it means that the customer or consumer can actually be part of the business application of every business in the world. The privacy issue—who can use detailed customer data to make one-to-one offerings—may finally be resolved when the consumer herself can take control over her profile and link it, wireless and in real time, to the Web. So, if a consumer does not want to be bothered, she can just log off for the moment or shut out a supplier for good.

The recurring theme of this book is reconnecting demand and supply using both innovation and efficiency improvement. Now, in Chapter 2, we start by looking at how more transparent demand has transformed supply chain management, and spawned the demand-supply chain.

■ REFERENCE

1. Jan Holmström, William E. Hoover Jr., Antti Vasara, and Perttu Louhiluoto, "The Other End of the Supply Chain," *McKinsey Quarterly*, No. 1, 2000, 63–79.

Chapter

Demand and Supply Chains—The New Supply Chain Management

The most difficult operations issue is how to offer better value to the customer and at the same time reduce costs.

■ SUPPLY CHAIN MANAGEMENT—STATE OF THE ART IN OPERATIONS

Supply chain management (SCM) has been successful in taking out inventory buffers and costs from the operations of manufacturers, distributors, and retailers. Companies participating in MIT's Integrated Supply Chain Management Program report impressive supply chain accomplishments. Companies have reduced inventory buffers by half, increased on-time deliveries by 40 percent, and reduced out-of-stock rates to a fraction while simultaneously doubling inventory turns.

Depending on the industry, Pittiglio Rabin Todd & McGrath (PRTM) found in its Integrated Supply Chain Benchmarking Study that best-practice supply chain management companies spend 3 percent to 7 percent less of their revenue on the supply chain than their median competitors. This cost efficiency directly improves the contribution margin, or provides an opportunity to permanently lower prices. In the grocery supply chain, the best-practice companies spend 5 percent less than the median. Here, a 5 percent increase in margins, or a permanently lower price level is tremendously important. The margin for the typical retailer is less than half the cost savings achieved by the best-practice supply chain management companies.

How have the best-practice companies achieved this? For a grocery manufacturer, the key to success has been to convince supply chain partners to adopt practices that enable the company to operate more efficiently.

Campbell Soup is a company that has successfully used pricing and process integration with customers as the tools to improve supply chain efficiency. How it works is pretty straightforward. First, the supplier defines a "best practice" for customers' purchasing that helps the supplier simplify processes and cut costs. Then, customers that follow best practice get a discount, and customers that don't follow the best practice are charged a surcharge. (And retailers are doing the same: Consumers buying from hypermarkets get discounts, while convenience customers pay a premium for saving time.)

In the Campbell Soup example, the discount is 10 cents per case for following best practice, and a 50-cent surcharge per case for inefficient purchasing practices. The best practice that gives the discount covers things such as buying full truck loads and full pallets directly from the plant, participating in a standard pallet exchange program, and using electronic data interchange for purchase orders and invoices.

The recipe to succeed differs between industries. In the grocery industry, the link between the supplier's pricing and retailers' and distributors' buying practices is key. That is, suppliers don't create higher supply chain costs by aggressive pricing promotions; instead, the aim is cost efficiency. In the personal computer (PC) industry, selling direct and assembling to order has proved an effective practice, while in yet other industries product design and supplier management may be critical for achieving bottom-line results in supply chain management.

Supply chain management incorporates the key ideas from lean manufacturing and supplier management, and extends the scope to distribution. The objective of supply chain management is to improve the efficiency of the product delivery process from materials suppliers all the way to the end customer—to get the right product, at the right time, to the end customer with a minimum of handling and buffering. The focus of improvement efforts is coordinating distribution, production, and purchasing across organizational units and different companies.

A key insight of supply chain management is that how products are made has a dramatic effect on distribution and the need to keep inventory buffers. A supplier that ships to order needs to keep an inventory of finished goods, and for each stock-keeping unit also have a safety stock to buffer against unexpected big orders.

A supplier that assembles to order can, in addition to eliminating the finished goods inventory, buffer against unexpected big orders on the product line level. This means that it does not matter which specific variety has bigger than expected demand, as long as there is free capacity and materials to assemble the ordered product. The result is improved flexibility to respond to changes in demand between the different product variants.

However, there is a trade-off between responsiveness and efficiency. For a supplier, it does not make sense to invest heavily in capacity and material buffers to reduce lost sales for products that have low margins. But, for high margin products it makes business sense (see Figure 2.1). Consider a branded product with a contribution margin of 50 percent. A stock-out rate of 20 percent, leading also to lost sales, reduces the contribution to profit and overhead by 10 percent (50% × 20% = 10%). Since this amount exceeds profits before taxes in many companies, responsiveness is a high priority for suppliers with high margin products. Compare this to a product with only a 10 percent contribution margin; here the same level of lost sales only reduces the contribution to profit and

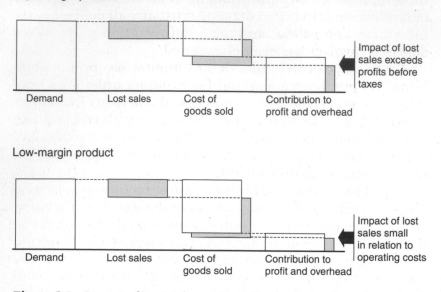

High-margin product

Demand Lost sales Cost of goods sold Contribution to profit and overhead

Impact of lost sales exceeds profits before taxes

Low-margin product

Demand Lost sales Cost of goods sold Contribution to profit and overhead

Impact of lost sales small in relation to operating costs

Figure 2.1 Impact of Lost Sales on Contribution to Profit and Overhead

overhead by 2 percent. In this situation, increasing responsiveness profitably is much more difficult, since increased sales are quickly offset by higher supply chain costs.

Marshall Fisher, of Pennsylvania's Wharton School, points out that depending on the contribution margin and the nature of demand[1] (Do stock-outs lead to lost sales? Is demand predictable?) companies need to consider different approaches for their supply chain design. For functional products, such as Campbell's soup, the best solution is an efficient supply chain. The primary purpose for an efficient supply chain is to fulfill predictable demand at the lowest possible cost. For innovative products, such as fashion wear, a responsive supply chain is the best match. The objective when building a market-responsive supply chain is to respond quickly to unpredictable demand to minimize lost sales, forced markdowns, and obsolescent inventory.

Since the early 1990s, Campbell Soup has been able to cut supply chain costs between 3 and 5 percent annually with an efficient supply chain strategy. But, today there is little more room for improvement when close to 95 percent of production is to actual demand, virtually all deliveries are full trucks and pallets, and the administration of paper orders and invoices has been eliminated.

On the responsive side, Dell Computer has been assembling and purchasing materials to customer order for a long time. A new development is merging the personal computer with its display in transit, and moving toward paying materials suppliers on shipment of the computer to the consumer. Here, also, the returns from further supply chain improvements are diminishing.

Demand, however, is a less recognized component in both efficient and responsive supply chain designs. For efficiency, a supplier needs to make demand more predictable; and for responsiveness to changing markets, a supplier needs to build relationships to consumers and business customers. The way forward is to focus on demand. Companies that have achieved what can be achieved through best practice in supply chain management continue to push back performance limits by recognizing the potential of the demand chain.

New technology such as the Internet, digital TV, and wireless is opening up completely new opportunities to do business. As a consequence, suppliers need to reassess established practices. In the computer and communications equipment industry companies like Dell and Cisco have already leveraged the Internet to build new effective channels for customer demand. In other industries, the development of new demand chains have just begun.

For example, various e-grocery business models have been tried out. Webvan replaced the supermarket with a logistics hub where customer orders are efficiently picked and dispatched. The pioneering company in business, Peapod, used existing supermarkets, picking and distributing from a supermarket near the consumer. And, Streamline has focused on building a long-term relationship with replenishment service to a special fridge for receiving groceries in the consumer's garage. Figure 2.2 shows the development, from the "serve yourself" model in the supermarket, to the "we service your home" model of Streamline.

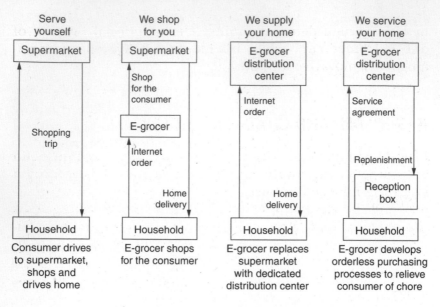

Figure 2.2 Grocery Business Models

In the past, products were displayed to the consumer primarily on supermarket shelves, but now display is on the Internet. Some products are not displayed at all, but are automatically replenished to the consumer's kitchen. For the supplier, a move from supermarket shelves to Web pages is not very dramatic, but if consumers don't purchase your product anymore—just have it automatically replenished— the change is dramatic. Traditional marketing and promotions won't work. Instead, you need to get the consumer to choose your product once and stay loyal.

Customers, even grocery consumers, are getting a wider choice in how they buy different products and services. The choice is not simply between purchasing from a traditional channel or the Internet, but also in different ways for buying, often without ordering.

The demand chain is the chain of activities through which the supplier recognizes customer demand. And, because customers with very different preferences may have demand for the supplier's product, the supplier must be able to differentiate demand chains. The functional product of one customer can, when offered and delivered appropriately, be innovative for another.

■ WHY DEMAND CHAIN MANAGEMENT?

How do you make the right offer to your customer, and avoid becoming a commodity supplier? Or worse yet, becoming a burden for locked-in customers? Having competitive products and the right supply chain for the average customer is not enough. Your supply chain has to be right for the individual customer as well. Here, the demand chain—the chain of activities that communicates demand from markets to suppliers—offers suppliers a wide range of opportunities to differentiate their value offering.

Understanding the demand chain is increasingly important as customers push for new and improved value from vendors:

➤ Focusing vendors on business outcomes for the customer (e.g., manufacturer buys lead time reduction from component supplier).

➤ Tying service level agreements to business processes (e.g., cycle time improvement).

➤ Insisting on pricing and packaging that allows the customer to share risk with the vendor (e.g., manufacturer wants to pay for components when shipping his own product).

In the electronics industry, responsive supply chains are critical for original equipment manufacturers. And, by asking component suppliers to manage in-plant stores of materials, the manufacturer can significantly improve order fulfillment lead times. (There is no need to wait for materials to arrive before assembling.)

The measurement division of Tektronix, Inc. pushed its five leading suppliers, All American Semiconductor, Avnet,

Insight Electronics, Marshall Industries, and Wyle Electronics into managing a common, single in-plant store in its assembly plant in Beaverton, Oregon.

Focusing on output is often linked to service level agreements that tie supplier performance to the customer's business process. In the Tektronix example, the suppliers are responsible for parts being available when needed; this even includes some custom parts. Essentially, the suppliers don't just provide a product, but perform a key service in the Tektronix operation: They are the supply managers. The suppliers don't fulfill orders, but respond to new product development, sales, and production planning processes of the customer.

But the push for new value is not limited to high-tech industry. In traditional retail operations, customers are already pressuring suppliers to carry inventory costs and share the risk of lost sales. The idea is "pay by scan," which means that suppliers are not paid for their goods until the consumer makes a purchase.

Conventional supply chain management (where you differentiate your processes by products) is no longer enough. It is necessary to focus on the customer's demand chain and on the value nets of different customers. Analyzing the demand chain helps the supplier better understand the customer's buying processes, and what drives them. Taking a step back to examine the value net, including the different roles and opportunities in a complex web of business relationships, allows a supplier to see how its value added depends on complementary service providers and competitors.

■ WHAT IS BEYOND THE CUSTOMER'S ORDER?

The purpose of demand chain management is giving the customer choice, not just a choice of product variety, but also of relationship. For your customer, you are the supplier, and he might very well want to manage what you do for him and make you a subcontractor, "just-in-time" supplier, or partner. But are you prepared; do you know how to approach the customer and how to vary your offering?

To be prepared, you need to integrate marketing into your operations. Supply chain management integrates purchasing, production, and distribution; it addresses how to make the products your customers buy and how to get the right components for these products. Demand chain management adds a new dimension. How do you build customer relationships, and how do you deliver value into the customer's operation?

This is a question of marketing, as well as supply chain management. Marketing is about understanding the customer's buying processes. The goal is to provide the customer with the right product, but also with the right service. Finding the right service—and providing this through production, sales, and distribution—is how marketing becomes part of demand-supply chain management.

To build the right customer relationship, the supplier needs to understand his customer's buying processes. What is the purpose for which the customer uses the supplier's product? Does the customer plan in advance where and how he will use the supplier's products? When does the customer use the product: Is use continuous and the customer maintains an inventory or installed base? How does the customer make the actual purchase decision? There are opportunities to be captured from understanding each step in the customer's demand chain, for example, purpose, planning, consumption, and purchasing (see Figure 2.3).

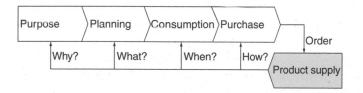

Figure 2.3 Go Beyond the Customer Order—Understand Your Customer's Purpose, Planning, and Consumption

➤ Why Does the Customer Order?

Why is it important to understand the purpose? It is quite obviously the key for improving the product itself to know how the end customer uses the product. But it is also essential for developing the supply chain to know how different customers, both consumers and intermediaries, use the product. A few examples can illustrate why the demand chains of different types of customers are important for supply chain innovation.

Many suppliers have large customer segments that do not use the product themselves. Some customers buy products from many different suppliers and distribute these to smaller customers. These customers—distributors and wholesalers—are sensitive to the risk of obsolescence, but are also very concerned about the supplier selling direct to their customers. There are also customers who sell to end users; they use the product for retailing. Here it is the profitability of retail space, be that grocery aisle or Web site, which is ultimately of greatest interest. Efficient Consumer Response—an improvement effort launched in the early 1990s by leading U.S. grocery suppliers to improve their relationships with their trade customers—is a good example of how a clear understanding of your customer's purpose can help you implement improvements that benefit both parties.

In the book supply chain where product variety is great and obsolescence costs are high, many distributors and retailers would welcome a publisher (or group of publishers) that could deliver their books through an effective print-on-demand solution. The point here is that while the end customer, the reader, might still want to purchase a printed book, intermediaries have different interests depending on their business purpose: They want to deliver a printed book, but not necessarily purchase it in the printed format.

A logistics service provider like United Parcel Service (UPS) might welcome a new supply chain design where the logistics service provider's role was expanded to printing and shipping books on demand from a number of different publishers directly to the consumers. Web-bookstores and smaller specialty retailers would also welcome such a service from the service provider as long as they get the sale (i.e., remain the interface to the book reader). However, for a larger traditional retailer, the preferred solution would be to make the sale and produce the book for the customer on the spot in the bookstore.

Another example is a supplier of enterprise resource planning (ERP) software for major corporations. In addition to the application, the supplier could also offer to operate their customers' systems. This would make it possible to reach smaller businesses with the same basic product, instead of creating a scaled-down version. This is also exactly what is happening. Companies such as SAP, Oracle, Peoplesoft, and Microsoft are all offering small, medium-size, and department-level business users advanced applications over the Web.

For end use, it is not only the product when purchased that matters but use over its life cycle. For end users, total cost of ownership might be what counts in the end. As the preceding examples demonstrate, it is not only the product that can be improved to increase value to the customer. The same can also be achieved by shifting the focus of the relationship.

➤ What Does the Customer Order?

Asking how, and if, the customer plans what products to use can also open up opportunities to add more value by changing the relationship. In the automotive industry, the car manufacturer systematically strives to get every important parts supplier to deliver according to the assembly schedule. However, the process starts with the car manufacturer deciding how a supplier's part will be used in the product design, sometimes transferring responsibility for a whole module (e.g., the interior including seats and upholstery) to the chosen supplier. Later, the rules and procedures for communicating assembly schedules and sequencing deliveries to the line are set. Sometimes, when the supplier delivers from in-plant stores, the final schedule can be frozen only minutes before the part is needed on the assembly line.

But all demand is not well managed, even in lean manufacturing operations. Your customer might be essential for you as a supplier, but for your customer you are just one of many alternative commodity suppliers. This situation gives the supplier opportunity to add value. Today, more and more large businesses and corporations plan how (standards) and when (validity periods) to use PCs. In Finland, one in 3 of the 50 largest corporations actively manage a corporatewide standard for PC hardware, software, and desktop. This was not always so, but cheaper hardware coupled with rising costs for PC support and maintenance have made managing standards a priority issue. For a supplier, actually delivering computers according to the customer's standard is only a half-baked solution. A supplier can best capture this business opportunity by developing support tools to help the customer manage standards more effectively and ensure that purchases are according to the standard. Dell's customized purchasing process (Premier Pages) combined with the Plus program for factory-installed, corporate-specific software is an example of such a value offering.

➤ When Does the Customer Order?

Does the customer use the product continuously (e.g., maintain an inventory or installed base)? This question also can open up new opportunities for the supplier. The customer might still want to use your product continuously, even though he is not ready to make the effort of planning. In practice, that means that the customer wants to maintain an inventory buffer, or an installed base.

For a customer maintaining an inventory buffer, the supplier has the opportunity to take responsibility for the customer's inventory, replenishing the customer instead of fulfilling the customer's purchase orders. To do this, new technology is often not needed. For example, a supplier of industrial gas found that for its large- and medium-size customers, demand was always stable for a subset of the company's products, and large enough to justify weekly delivery. Simply identifying these products together with the customer made it possible to offer weekly replenishments, and reduce the work in purchasing and inventory management for that customer. The regular visits by the delivery truck, in turn, made it possible to extend replenishment to smaller stock-keeping units using a two-bin system. For the items that the delivery truck does not always replenish, the driver simply records which low volume products now are on their last unit and need replenishing the next time over.

In the case of a customer maintaining an installed base, the opportunity is to streamline the service or replacement of a unit. Consider, for example, a local consulting company using mobile phones. Every one in a consulting position and many in the support staff traveling a lot must have a mobile phone continuously. This is an opportunity for a retail chain to offer immediate replacement of a broken or lost phone from any retail outlet in the country for the employees of the consulting company. Similarly, companies leasing cars to businesses have developed streamlined processes to provide replacement cars in case of problems and breakdowns.

➤ How Does the Customer Order?

The major unexplored opportunities for a supplier are linked to the purpose, planning, and consumption steps in the customer demand chain. The reason is that supplier companies have rarely looked closely at what is behind the customer order. However, there is also opportunity from understanding how the customer makes the actual order. The customer may ask for competing bids, alternate between certified suppliers, or simply buy from whoever has the cheapest price. In such situations, the opportunity lies in helping the customer buy better.

A manufacturer may want to consolidate purchases over different business units and sites. The reason is that the company wants to maximize its buyer power to obtain volume discounts, or through process standardization make use of discounts offered by suppliers to best-practice customers. The next level of sophistication is a customer that partners with other organizations through an intermediary. This aggregates demand not only over business units within a corporation, but across corporations.

Even though the customer objective is to increase buying power, it does not have to mean lower margins for the supplier. When business units and different organizations aggregate demand, it can give the supplier access to new customers. But even when no new customers are reached, there are opportunities for the supplier. The key for the supplier is to ensure that the aggregation of demand can make the supply chain more efficient, and that the supplier can secure part of that efficiency improvement. To match the aggregation of demand, suppliers will increasingly need to collaborate with other suppliers, or third-party logistics service providers, to achieve the required efficiency improvements.

In the 1990s, Procter & Gamble, Campbell Soup, and other leading suppliers in the grocery supply chain achieved cost reductions by encouraging customers to aggregate demand from more retail locations. And, keeping a stable price level also encourages customers to deliver the product more frequently to the point of sales from the customer's distribution centers. It is an aggregation of demand over locations, not over time.

The opportunity for the supplier in online bidding is in developing transparent responsiveness. When the supplier responds to a customer request for a quote on a customized design, the key information is price, quantity, and aggregate lead time. This, however, does not yet make it possible for the customer to assess what the delivery accuracy will be. But if the supplier has tuned his supply chain for responsiveness—not only claiming responsiveness—he can give details on how the timing of the customer order and other inputs translate to project milestones and a delivery schedule. Based on this, the customer can appraise the capability of the supplier to deliver to promise and monitor progress once the deal is made. So, the supplier opportunity is not only an offer of the requested product but also a transparent process to deliver it on schedule.

It is critical to note the role of quality in online bidding, where an intermediary streamlines the purchasing and sales transaction by guiding the customer to the best available supplier. The key task for the intermediary is not to administrate the bidding process, but to identify and screen supply. The assessment of product quality is a prerequisite for success. Many early electronic markets failed because customers did not trust quality. For example, the Information Auctioning system for potted plants launched by Blomenveiling Aalsmer in Holland in 1994 failed. The reason was that customers did not trust the sample lots used to represent the main supply. On the other hand, AUCNET, a used car auction introduced in Japan in 1986 has succeeded. The intermediary set up a rigorous process to assess the quality of used cars offered by the sellers, which saved on the interaction cost of negotiation and assessment for the customer. Today, AUCNET is listed on the Tokyo Stock Exchange with expected sales of JPY 13.25 billion in 2000.

Current e-commerce developments have barely scratched the surface of opportunity. The demand chain deals not only with how the customer makes the purchase, but also with what drives the customers' purchasing transactions. Going beyond the transaction opens new opportunities that the bulk of e-commerce developments have not yet touched. You can collaborate on many different levels: streamlining the trading process, maintaining the customer's inventory or installed base, planning when and what supplies are needed, and even transforming the product supplier role into a service provider role.

The demand chain links marketing to planning and control, as well as to supplier management. This linkage can be very valuable. A supplier needs to react to changes in product range, pricing, and promotions—the things the supplier does himself that change demand, or that the customer does. For example, sales makes a special offer to win over a new large customer. In many companies, this immediately creates a potential problem situation because sales does not worry about how the additional demand can and should be met. If the news reaches operations only through requirements planning, and there are no links to existing customers' planning, it will be very difficult to respond to both the new and existing customers according to their expectations. If the new customer stays, operations won't ever know what hit them, only that demand suddenly changed. And if the customer is unhappy with the service level, and does not stay, operations only saw a sudden spike in demand that disappeared when ignored.

Even though it can be expensive for the supplier to change the value offering to the customer, offering value earlier in the demand chain gives the supplier more time to react. Offering PCs according to corporate standards is a good example. The supplier's corporate accounts know the schedule of the customer decision-making process, and know that the customer's standard is not likely to be changed before the next planned update of the standards. This understanding of the customer's demand chain can then be used to make more reliable forecasts on the component level, which is very useful when negotiating with component suppliers. For critical components, the PC supplier can early on ensure that its supply will be sufficient, and component suppliers get reliable and early indication on future demand.

■ WHAT IS YOUR VALUE ADDED?

Going beyond the customer order helps you spot opportunities to improve your value added in absolute terms. But it does not tell you much about your value added in relation to competitors, other suppliers, and third parties, nor how deeper collaboration with the customer would affect the competitive situation. How do you then assess your total competitive value added and the potential for collaboration?

Adam Brandenburger and Barry Nalebuff introduce a practical approach for this in their book *Co-opetition*.[2] The starting position is to view business as a game, and to model who the players are and what their roles are as a value net. The value net around a business consists of customers, suppliers, competitors, and complementors. The result is a bird's-eye view of your company. The crucial difference between the classic supply chain and the value net perspectives is that in the value net you also consider your competition and complementors (Figure 2.4).

In the value net, a player is your complementor if customers value your service more when they also have the other player's service than when they have your service alone. A simple example is the mobile phone: It needs a network operator to be useful. But you can apply the same logic to analyzing improvement potentials in the customer relationship. For example, retailers value a supplier that has an electronic order processing solution more if it has the same transaction interface as other suppliers (e.g., VAN, EDI, Web).

A competitor is the mirror image of a complementor—customers value your service less when they have the other player's service. For example, a supplier can offer many different solutions to reduce a retailer's transaction and supply chain costs. One solution is for suppliers to directly

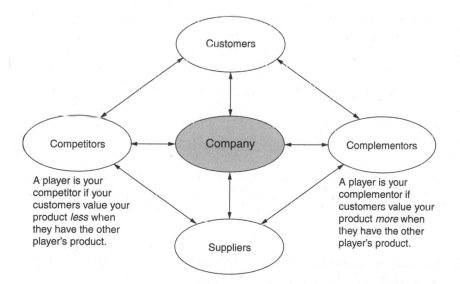

Figure 2.4   The Value Net Expands the Supply Chain View to Competitors and Complementors

replenish the retail stores based on point-of-sales reports; another is for the supplier to manage the inventory level in a distribution hub. In the latter case, retailers keep sending orders to a distribution hub. A retailer, however, can perceive the solutions as substitutes. A retailer that already has many suppliers replenishing its distribution hub would show little interest in a solution for replenishing the stores directly proposed by a new supplier. Here, every player replenishing the distribution hub is a competitor for the supplier with the solution to replenish stores directly.

The links in the value net go in both directions, so there is another side to the story. It is not only the company that has competitors and complementors. The customer also has competitors and complementors in relation to the company. Here, a complementor for a customer is a player that makes it more attractive for the company to provide resources to serve the customer. In Denmark, Frode Laursen A/S is a third-party logistics provider that handles the distribution to the retail shops for both local and multinational packaged consumer goods manufacturers. Fierce rivals like Unilever and Procter & Gamble can be complementors in the relationship between the company (Frode Larsen) and the customers (the retail shops). The more manufacturers that use the third-party logistics provider, the more attractive it is for the third party to improve its distribution systems.

How do you assess your value added in the value net? Your value added is the size of the total pie with you "in" minus the size of the pie with you "out." The PC distributors in the United States faced this question when mass customization and direct sales proved to be a highly successful business model. Would this mean that the total pie would be bigger without distributors, and that distributors were on the way out?

To decide the issue in their favor, the distributors needed a way to increase the size of the pie. The solution was that distributors took over some assembly and coordination tasks from the manufacturers and this way increased the value added by more than 5 percent. Channel assembly carries similar costs to supplier build-to-stock, and may even be slightly cheaper in some cases. On the other hand, channel assembly reduces markdown costs—price erosion—in the distribution channel by typically 5 percent, in addition to reducing lost sales in the retail stores (see Figure 2.5).

Another view on the value added of different channel members can be seen in Cisco's decision to keep delivering its products to network operators through the traditional channels, also after having set up an online sales channel. Here, retailers, local sales organizations, and systems integrators do not sell the product anymore—demand is captured directly through Cisco's online sales—but delivery of products, on-site services, and support is still through the traditional channels. The result is a business configuration where Cisco now controls the demand chain from the operator customer, but still uses the existing channels with intermediaries to deliver full value to the operator customers.

Why is it important to understand your value added in relation to all players in the value net? It is because you as a supplier can have a better solution and because the customer is not always right—or not the only one who is right. The demand chain can then be used to change the scope, and to identify opportunities to increase value added.

Grocery retailers have traditionally focused on reducing the cost of goods sold to improve profitability. Consequently, suppliers taking the customer seriously respond

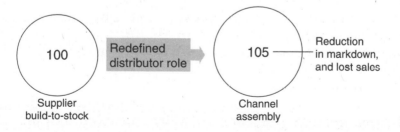

Figure 2.5 Distributor Can Increase the Pie by Doing Mass-Customization in the Traditional Chain

with promotions and discounts to win more business. In the past decade, however, suppliers have succeeded in winning more business without promotions and discounts. How is this done? The first step is to put yourself in the shoes of the customer to identify the full demand chain. This is the way to start changing the relationship, to give it a new scope.

In the Efficient Consumer Response initiative, development efforts in the grocery industry moved to collaboration. The key insight was to understand that retailer profitability depends more on better service to the consumer than on purchasing cost. The next step was to correctly demonstrate how transaction and handling costs, obsolescence and lost sales, and capital tied up in inventory directly affect the retailer's profitability. Once the costs of wastage, obsolescence, inventory, and handling in the chain were highlighted, it became easier to determine how a supplier by replenishing more efficiently, and now increasingly by collaborating on planning and forecasting, could add more value. It is this first step—taking a point of view other than your own—that is the difficult one and the one that gives insights.

Can the customer collect all the benefits of an improved solution by playing the supplier out against competitors (i.e., does it pay off for the customer to risk the relationship)? In theory, online purchasing makes it easier for a customer to play a supplier out against competitors. But, because standards for content and transaction management do not exist yet, a substantial cost still is involved in starting doing business with a new supplier.

In essence, this is the same old problem that Electronic Data Interchange (EDI) encountered. Passing orders and invoices is easy, but managing product data and definitions is difficult. When analyzing product information in customer purchasing systems, suppliers often find wrong or outdated information in up to a third of the items. Product catalogs may be a solution, but the catalog information affects the type of purchasing process that is possible. All in all, the opportunity for customers to press for lower prices is balanced by the cost savings from dealing with a supplier that is well tuned to the customer's demand chain.

CHALLENGE THE RULES OF THE GAME

The traditional supply chain for photocopier and laser printer paper—a simple supply chain where a paper mill, wholesaler, distributor, and retailer make decisions on purchasing and production in response to demand from their respective customer—can be used to demonstrate how demand is distorted by uncoordinated decisions.

However, it can also be used to show how the rules of the game prompt players to make bad decisions. The key is that there is a penalty for every missed unit of delivery (not being able to get the product immediately will make the customer turn to an alternative supplier) as well as costs for every unit of inventory. The supply chain for Copier Paper is:

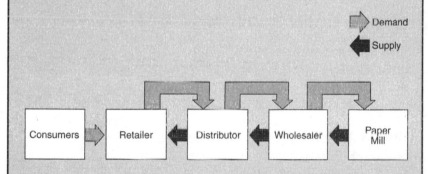

The penalty for every unit of missed delivery prompts players to react strongly toward shortages and increase their orders. The chain of events is set off by the retailer when demand increases and the retailer increases his order to cover both the increase in demand and the reduction of his safety stock. If the distributor and the wholesaler also do the same (i.e., increase orders to match the customer demand and to rebuild safety buffers), then the paper mill will not be able to deliver enough.

The result is that there appear to be penalties—lost sales—from missed deliveries. But assuming there are capacity constraints, the lost sales are only temporary movements of inventory between different players. For the customer—

(continued)

CHALLENGE THE RULES OF THE GAME (CONTINUED)

any customer, be it wholesaler, distributor, or retailer—the only real penalty for a missed delivery is when the retailer cannot sell to the consumer.

When asked for improvement suggestions, people involved in the supply chain rarely see that abolishing the penalty for missing deliveries to fill up safety stock is a huge opportunity to improve the supply chain. Also, participants rarely question why orders are needed. Instead, improvement suggestions usually keep the basic rules in place, but add an element of interaction between the retailer and the manufacturer.

"End-to-end" interaction is fine in theory, but the practical problem is, What happens when the manufacturer has to interact with hundreds of retailers instead of one? In that case, it is worth considering if it would not be more efficient to change the rules—the penalty that prompts players to exaggerate demand—rather than add more tasks to coordinate the chain. A practical way for the supplier to do this is to change the value offering: Instead of order fulfillment, the offering can also be availability to the customer's customer.

Even in the online world, a supplier can offset competition by tuning in better to the customer's demand chain. But, is it then only the online complementors, such as product catalog publishers, that are in the position to collect substantial benefits from increased business collaboration by positioning themselves between customers and suppliers? No, not necessarily. Suppliers can become complementors themselves. The Boston e-grocer Streamline has pioneered a system for unattended receipt of goods in the consumer's home. The special refrigerator it installs in the garage of the customer contains three compartments for different temperatures and can also be locked. By offering to deliver products for other suppliers through its distribution system, Streamline can become a key complementor for a wide range of services, such as video rentals, dry cleaning, and parcel delivery.

■ BUILD THE DEMAND-SUPPLY CHAIN TO COMPETE COLLABORATIVELY

A supplier that is continuously pushed by the customer to lower price can sometimes escape the trap by suggesting that closer collaboration will provide significant new benefits in the future. The potential for developing a profitable customer relationship improves if the relationship can be made continuous, for example, by making the supplier's role for reducing total costs of ownership transparent.

In a transactional customer-supplier relationship, the classic trio of product, price, and promotion are the key factors differentiating suppliers. In a collaborative relationship, customer demand beyond the individual customer orders becomes an operational concern for the supplier.

For example, how can the customer's business be operated more efficiently and responsively by purchasing continuously from the supplier? Dell Computer is very careful to make its relationship with corporate customers collaborative. When corporate customers pointed out that ordering online is fine, but it really just transferred order administration and call center tasks from the supplier to the customer, Dell responded by adding features that simplified tasks for the customer. Among the added features, the register over computers in use in the corporation simplifies accounting, and the customer can use the online shipment report for easy invoice verification.

Equipment registers and shipment reports are both straightforward extensions of the traditional order fulfillment process. But, are simple add-on features enough? When the payoff from risking future developments is higher than that of continuing the collaboration, the relationship is in danger.

Trust becomes an issue in building collaborative relationships when there is a temptation to get big-shot term benefits. A short supply of hot products, or an oversupply of outdated ones, are typical situations where big temptations can scuttle the collaboration.

In the high-tech area, the temptation is often for a supplier to push products that risk becoming obsolete. For the customer, the temptation is to withhold information on demand to secure higher shares of products in short supply. For the supply chain as a whole, the optimal solution would be for both parties to collaborate—to ramp up and down products in a controlled manner together. However, implementing solutions that support smooth product introductions becomes difficult. For a supplier of mobile phones, it is very tricky to implement vendor managed inventory with channel partners, when demand for a new model exceeds supply by several hundred percent. In such a situation, guaranteeing availability for a new product to one channel partner can mean that the available product goes to that one customer with serious repercussions on other customer relationships.

For contract assemblers in the electronics industry, responsiveness is key. The contract manufacturer needs to be able to assemble new products, for new customers on short notice. In this situation, component distributors can simplify the task considerably. Making sure that all required materials are available when assembly is scheduled is difficult if materials are planned and delivered on an item-by-item basis. To resolve this issue, component distributors, such as Avnet, offer to deliver material kits according to the bill of materials. Another form of building the collaborative relationship is in-plant stores, from which the contract manufacturer simply withdraws materials as needed.

The customer benefits by obtaining much simplified and more responsive processes. For the supplier, the benefit is more predictable and stable demand, as well as more business, and a premium for the value-added services. In this situation, it is even possible for competitors to work together. A good example of such a collaborative network around a customer is the Tektronix example presented earlier in this chapter. There, five leading suppliers set up a common in-plant store in the customer operation.

Once you get going, there is positive feedback and increasing returns with a built-in bias toward ever-closer partnership and specialization, or to use a term from biology—coevolution. The value added, and costs of replacement make the threshold for abandoning a collaborative solution higher. A company that has successfully outsourced value-adding operations outside its core competency has a difficult time taking that back later. The reason is simple: A good partner has improved its ability to provide value, while the company that outsourced has fallen behind. For example, IBM with all its resources was not able to successfully launch a competing operating system for PCs, when it wanted to reverse its decision to use Microsoft's product.

Likewise, successful network arrangements migrate toward long-term collaboration if the costs of assembling new networks are significant. The value net around Windows, and Intel in the PC business is the classic example of increasing returns in action.

A company that has competed with consultative sales and that blindly commits itself to the best-practice benchmark and creates a new direct e-sales channel to business customers—without understanding what its value added is in relation to other players—takes a huge risk to commoditize itself. The danger is that the company can easily be exploited as a commodity supplier if existing value-adding links to the customer are severed. By selling products directly over the Web it changes the relationship from continuous to transactional.

But collaboration also has risks. Focusing on the most demanding customers can lure a supplier into building up a business model that does not work with less demanding customers. For example, a castings supplier developing its operations according to the requirements of an automotive original equipment manufacturer (OEM) may find that its new business model only works effectively when all the customers give advance schedule and frequent call off orders.

The positive feedback is now to seek more automotive customers and drop more traditional buyers. Increased dependency is the flip side of collaboration.

The most effective way to collaborate competitively is by focusing on your customer's demand chain and developing capabilities to add value in the different stages of demand, to coevolve with the customer on multiple levels. The difficult task, however, is to do this with a large number of partners, and different demand chains, while both the competition and the customers change. For this, you need to stop thinking in classic terms of either demand or supply chain management, and combine the two: You must manage your demand-supply chains in an evolving value net.

■ OBJECTIVES OF DEMAND-SUPPLY CHAIN MANAGEMENT

The primary objective of demand-supply chain management is to increase your value added to the customer, while improving asset performance and cost efficiency also from a customer perspective.

Marshall Industries, the electronics component distributor, doubled its revenue between 1994, when the company started scaling up its value-added offerings, and 1998, when value-added services reached 50 percent of sales. At the same time, cost efficiency and responsiveness improved by replacing conventional EDI links with Web applications, and ordering with collaborative forecasting and planning. Where forecast accuracy was once only 40 percent, it soon approached 65 percent.

Key elements in achieving the demand-supply chain management objectives of simultaneous growth, efficiency, and responsiveness are:

➤ Make customer relationships collaborative.
➤ Offer value interactively.
➤ Be aware of positive feedback that can both drive and erode your value added in the value net.

➤ Target offerings at distinct points in the customer demand chains.

➤ Drive efficiency improvements also through marketing.

➤ Package successful offerings from lead customers to reach smaller customers.

To make the customer relationship continuous, the supplier must be able to point at future benefits from collaboration. At its simplest, it is a matter of customer loyalty schemes and rewarding of repeat purchases. A more elaborate approach is to make service agreements, focusing on outcomes in the customer operations, such as reduced total cost of ownership.

Why aim for an "interactive offering" in a continuous relationship? An important reason is to make your offering harder for competitors to copy. Reactive (customized) and proactive (mass customized) offerings are easy to copy. Just consider Dell's interactive offering to load company-specific software on the PCs in the assembly plant; it is much more difficult to match than an offering to load a configuration of standard software, or to send after-sales support to load the software at the customer's office.

When developing new value offerings it is important to be aware of positive feedback loops. These loops can improve the value added; for example, a supplier by synchronizing closely with a big customer, gets a more level demand, which improves service to all customers, which allows synchronization with more customers. But positive feedback can also go the other way. Bad delivery service leads to one customer building up safety buffers, which distorts demand, and makes it more difficult for the supplier to deliver accurately, which prompts more customers to build up buffers, and so on.

Integrate different sources of value (e.g., product, availability, customization, aftersales service) into offerings aimed at distinct points in the customer demand chains, not according to customer segments. Focusing on different points in the demand chain results in offerings becoming more modular. A corporate customer using mobile phones either plans purchases for new employees or not, and a car manufacturer installing phones in new cars either purchases to plan, or replenishes a buffer. It is highly beneficial to focus on offering better value to customers that plan, manage inventory, or search for bargains if you have a lot of customer segments. This helps you get a wider coverage, with fewer solutions, compared with segment-specific developments because you can use the same solution elements over and over in the different segments.

Drive efficiency improvements also through marketing, not process reengineering alone. Rolling out is also selling in! You need to accept that supply chain efficiency improvements must be realized by changing relationships customer by customer. It took Procter & Gamble well over 10 years to reach 40 percent of volume for their efficient replenishment model. Just collaborating with a few customers might not give an immediate boost to your own efficiency, but by incrementally increasing coverage through marketing the benefits of collaboration to customers you can step-by-step, take out more supply chain buffers.

Standardize successful value offerings made to lead customers—that is, make SKU-like-to reach smaller customers. For example, Dell built up its relationship business model serving business customers, but by transferring elements of the relationship model—like virtual key account managers—on an Internet platform it has now been able also to reach individual consumers with value-added offerings. Another example is SAP, the Enterprise Resource Planning (ERP) software giant. By packaging implementation best practices, such as implementation process and support services, the company has been able to better reach midsize businesses, and by developing application hosting services together with Sun even small companies can be reached.

How to offer better value to the customer while reducing costs and improving supply chain efficiency is the most difficult operations issue. New technology, such as mobile and electronic business applications, supply chain synchronization packages, and self-service applications are not a panacea. To benefit from technology, you need first to understand your customer's demand chains and your value added (i.e., learn how to collaborate with your customer to compete more efficiently). The topic of the next chapter is how to leverage the demand-supply chain for value innovation.

■ REFERENCES

1. Marshall Fisher, "What Is the Right Supply Chain for Your Product?" *Harvard Business Review,* March–April 1997, 105–116.
2. Adam Brandenburger and Barry Nalebuff, *Co-opetition,* New York: Doubleday, 1996.

Chapter 3

Value Thresholds and Traps

You can compete better by collaborating: Improving the value offering to your customer helps you operate more effectively yourself.

■ THE CONCEPT OF A VALUE INNOVATION

Making a distinction between technological innovation and value innovation is typical for companies that redefine their markets and escape the rat race for competitive advantage. W. Chan Kim[1] and Reneé Mauborgne, professors at the management school INSEAD in France, have found that companies that focus on the customer relationship and how to deliver value to the customer are able to consistently grow faster and more profitably. Rather than building advantages over their competitors, value-innovating companies make competition irrelevant by providing buyers a quantum leap in value (value innovation). The focus of strategy shifts from the competition to the customer.

Technology-oriented companies, such as Ford, IBM, Intel, Microsoft, Dolby, Cisco, and Nokia, have been acknowledged as masters in creating competitive bundles of products and services. In this book, however, we are not focusing on competitive advantage based on product leadership. We focus on the customer relationship as a key dimension in uncovering value innovations in the demand-supply chain.

Our scope starts where the realm of competitive products and services ends. We focus on capturing new business opportunities by setting up customer-supplier relationships for particular situations instead of offering particular products or services.

The concept of value innovation refers to the customer's valuation of the supplier's value offering. A value innovation is not just any value offering proposed to the customer. Instead, a value innovation gives the customers a quantum leap in value. For the demand-supply chain, we define value threshold this way:

> *A value threshold is a supplier value offering that produces a quantum improvement in the operations and performance of the customer.*

Accordingly, a customer perceives a new value offering that does not enable him to redefine his own operation and performance as just "business as usual" among the competing suppliers. A value innovation is a distinct offering that makes it possible for the customer to change the way he operates. It is the starting point of a coevolutionary process where both the customer and supplier can uncover new sources of value thanks to the changes made by the other party. As a result, the customer starts to assign higher value to the particular supplier's offering because of the value it adds to the customer's business. Once a value threshold is reached, the customer gets "locked on" to the supplier and the process is difficult to stop or reverse.

In particular, e-business opportunities in the marketplace give a supplier company new tools to integrate complementary offerings into the customer specific demand-supply chains from the wider business networks. This way e-business serves as a catalyst for closer collaboration, not only in a single customer-supplier relationship but also over the whole value net, including complementors and even competitors.

The e-business technologies have created a vast realm of opportunities for value innovation, though technology is just one of the practical constraints you need to consider when looking for opportunities to change the operation and performance of your customer. The key is to know where and how to use the technology to start building more effective collaborative business models and practices.

The demand-supply chain opens up ample opportunities as Dell, IKEA, and Home Depot have demonstrated. The objective in this elaboration is to understand and explain why and how the customer's behavior really may change. The fundamental question is to ask how some players with commodity products succeeded in becoming the preferred choice for a large number of customers. A good starting point is to consider Dell Computer, the star of the PC business, which throughout the 1990s gained market share—not so much due to offering superior products—but by focusing on making the purchasing process significantly more streamlined and easy for the customer.

In the demand-supply chain, the sources of value innovation can be understood from three different angles:

1. Reshaping the customer relationship.
2. Taking a new perspective on costs.
3. Extending delivery to fulfillment.

The three points of view are interrelated: If a supplier can make an inroad in one dimension, chances are that he can build on the first value innovation with other ways to transform both his customer's and his own demand-supply chain. If the supplier is able to change the relationship so that the customer entrusts the supplier with more information, the supplier can make purchasing and after sales more streamlined, or convenient. The convenience translates into time savings that reduce total costs; if the setup allows the customer to personalize the bundle of goods and services, we have a fulfillment model that the supplier can efficiently scale up to whole customer segments.

Since we are somewhat biased toward e-business related value innovation, this chapter focuses on new evolving business models.

■ RESHAPING THE CUSTOMER RELATIONSHIP

Reshaping the customer relationship is the first approach we can take to unravel value innovation in the demand-supply chain. Value innovation based on changing the customer relationship can take many forms. In this section, we analyze three practical approaches to impact the customer operation and improve the supplier operation:

1. Convenience of buying.
2. Customization and personalization.
3. Complementing of offerings.

➤ Convenience of Buying

What is the customer experience when using e-business channels rather than traditional models? Figure 3.1 sums up consumer response.

The primary reason for preferring an e-business model above a traditional marketplace is the convenience of shopping. Each time that a consumer can save time by making a purchase with a few key strokes online, instead of hopping in the car to go to the store or calling up the supplier by phone,

Top 5 Motivations
Convenience
Ease of research
Good prices/deals
Good selection/availability
Fun

Figure 3.1 Rationality toward E-business—The Consumer Viewpoint According to Forrester Research

is a valuable gain for someone spending a lot of time in cyberspace. Travelocity and Amazon, the leaders in their respective fields, have consistently invested in the convenience of shopping. Both aim to collect a full range of products and services in their industry and provide a unified use interface, access to real-time availability data, and one keystroke purchasing routines. They both also provide facilities for the customer to research available alternatives. And as the alternatives seem to be rich in depth and breadth, few potential customers feel a need to explore other marketplace sites.

In business-to-business commerce, industrial customers literally have a cost attached to their own time expenditure. Here, what can be saved from purchasing routines can be put to more productive use elsewhere (e.g., in the improving service and quality to the customer, or solving the customer's problems).

Ease of research, which is quoted as the number two motivation to buy online, is simply another aspect of convenient buying. Online, a supplier can provide a rich amount of data, test reports, and so on to the customer. However, both in providing the customer with information and in streamlining the buying process the relationship is pivotal. The value innovation is not the online service itself, but changing the relationship so that the supplier continuously makes it easier for the customer to find the product or service needed and do the purchase.

The trick is to customize the amount and flavor of customer-directed communication. The customer selects what he or she considers the best choice, typically without any intermediaries. This is also the way to compensate for gaps in sales personnel competencies. One salesperson might be an expert on technical product specifications while another has devoted his attention to aftermarket services. With online support, sales and aftermarket services can be considerably more competent on both dimensions. Thus, convenient buying is related to customization, complementing offerings, and total cost of ownership.

A fundamental point about value innovation is that while the business model can be copied, there is a first mover advantage because a relationship always requires time for developing, and changing what has become a habit is inconvenient for the customer.

The first fast-response photo shops could cherry-pick the locations for the new service, and latecomers were forced to try to break the established buying process of the consumer. An established buying process is also the key first-mover advantage in e-business related value innovation. If a bookstore anywhere in the world considers going into e-business today, it cannot even dream about establishing the same convenience as global e-bookstores like Amazon.com, which leads the pack with a customer relationship that has lasted perhaps for years. The entrant may provide the same standard functionality for search and purchasing, but is at a serious disadvantage in applying it. Instead of a competitive attack, the bookstore may do better to stay offline and seek opportunities in the domain of bundles of goods and services, cost, quality, and delivery, beyond what online players can offer.

An important aspect of leveraging the customer relationship for value innovation through increasing the convenience of buying is to understand that your customer can also be your supplier. In the Scandinavian automobile business, it has long been common practice for the new car dealers to buy the customer's used car as partial payment for a new vehicle. Even though the used car market is very price competitive, consumers are often highly confused about the gross margin the dealer receives from selling the used car and the price the customer receives. This confusion can easily lead to suspicions about paying too much for a new car, and getting too little for the old one.

The current solution is to make transparent the different pricing policies for customers trading in their old car and customers purchasing a new vehicle. A new value innovation is car dealerships that set up a two-way channel where customers can hunt for the best deal on both their old and new car. Autobytel has created such a marketplace to leverage the two-way customer-seller relationship. Customers can compare different trade-in options, to ensure that they receive a fair price for the old car. The pricing becomes transparent, reducing consumers' confusion. Naturally, the value innovation lies in recognizing the customer relationship and giving customers the opportunity to get the market price for the used car.

➤ Customization and Personalization

Customization and personalization are often the keys to value innovation in the customer relationship. The basic principle is that if the relationship can be customized and personalized, the need for traditional market segmentation disappears. (Instead you may need to segment based on customers' experience or on how well they can serve themselves.)

Levi's Personal Pair pilot, launched in 1994, is a good example of how to establish a new continuous relationship by providing customized products. The consumer just needs to provide the supplier with the critical measurements of inseam, waist, and so on, and the delivery address. For many consumers, this opens up a whole new world: No longer is it necessary to repeat the same procedures every time for measuring and making changes. And the supplier, and retailer can greatly reduce the risk of obsolescence and lost sales when making the jeans to order. Based on the experience from the pilot, Levi's launched the Original Spin™ program in 1998. In locations that carry the customized jeans, sales volumes have doubled and, in some cases, tripled.

Customization and personalization do not automatically lead to a change in customer relationships. Fiat has gone one step further than Levi's in the customization and personalization process. A recent model, Fiat Ecobasic, can literally be customized in the dealership. But the novelty in Fiat's solution is the delivery process, not the customer relationship. Fiat assembly plants ship the product skeletons and the option kits separately to car dealers. Based on the customer specification, the car dealer's personnel carry out the final assembly of the cars in the dealership. Whether this will prove to be a true value innovation depends on how well this embedded product design and delivery concept can be used to also change the customer relationship.

For the supplier, it is pivotal that customers start to serve themselves. In many collaborative self-service processes implemented with e-business technology, a remarkable logic of scalability becomes evident. When consumers carry out all actions in order entry and product configuration over the Internet application provided by the supplier, the workload for the supplier is practically unrelated to the order volume (at least in terms of the efforts needed for order entry, shipping documents, and invoicing).

The beauty of self-service on the Web is that it makes it possible to capture a vast number of one-to-one relationships through self-service personalization and customization. If the personalized product or service can be distributed in a digital format, the whole order-delivery process is highly scalable. However, when physical products are personalized and shipped to consumers one by one, the actual production and shipping operations only seldom are scalable, and create a whole new set of performance demands on the suppliers.

How do you get customers to design their own service and spend time and effort to maintain a relationship with the supplier? Self-service planning and configuration aids for the customers are not panacea, but have to be applied with caution. In the worst case, the supplier offering to the customer is merely an attempt to force the customer to think the producer's way. In such an approach, customers are forced to make a trade-off between their own convenience and the competitiveness of that particular supplier's products; they sacrifice their best performance to improve the performance of the supplier. In a win-win approach, however, the supplier makes the new offering with customers' business processes in mind, very much in the spirit of quality function deployment. The potential payoff for the supplier is a premium as customers reward sincere efforts to improve their performance. Thus, the clue for value innovation is a deeper understanding of the customer-supplier relationship (i.e., what is behind the order in the customers' demand chain).

Cisco is an excellent example. Gradually, they have introduced more and more self-service functionality in their customer services and thereby integrated their activities with customers' daily operations. These services are layered in such a way that key customers are using extended services while spot shoppers live with something less powerful. Cisco makes clear to new customers how using the provided service adds value. Therefore customers outside the inner circle are drawn to a more permanent relationship, exactly according to the intentions of Cisco.

It is not only a curiosity that Cisco is following the footprint of IKEA in the traditional channel by letting customers carry out some of the tasks (like configuration) typically dedicated to the supplier rather than the customer. The point is that self-service is a cost-efficient way to customize and personalize the customer-supplier relationship.

Some producers allow their customers to load and schedule their facilities. Such a collaborative procedure is an example of a value innovation in supply chain planning and control. Many printed circuit board assembly companies allow their customers (typically electronics product integrators) to exercise remote control of the supplier's production lines. These relationships hold sometimes for internal, sometimes for external, customers or both. The benefit for the customer is flexibility and efficiency in prioritizing and rescheduling expensive key components; for the circuit board supplier, it is an effective way to give the customer the best possible service under the circumstances.

➤ Complementing Offerings

As many corporations concentrate ever more heavily on their core competence areas, they become more and more dependent on outside suppliers and service providers. To offer customers an attractive bundle of products and services, the company needs increasingly to leverage its value net, and the strengths of its complementors. A company may uncover many opportunities for value innovation when it realizes that the customer relationship is not only between the supplier and the customer, but between the supplier, its complementors, and the customers.

Outsourcing is part of creating a complementing offering. Outsourcing entails a simplification of the supplier operation to improve its cost competitiveness, as well as the creation of a more complex collaborative demand chain to improve the customer relationship and integrate complementor's offerings. It requires that products and services provided by the complementor are properly integrated as an offering that fits the customer demand, or that the customer does the integration himself or herself.

For example, GE Locomotive started as an OEM product supplier and has expanded its competencies and service offering downstream to provide a full range of services including financing and aftermarket services. The company even offers to operate the locomotives for the customer. Today, customers value such a comprehensive set of services not only because it simplifies their own operations, but because it also reduces the headcount for the payroll.

However, the need to leverage the value net for complementing offerings is most evident after the customer has purchased the product. For most technical products, aftermarket service is a must. In those businesses where aftermarket service is one of the key purchasing criteria, assembling a complementing offering in the market operations can be a value innovation.

Boeing is a major manufacturing company that has extensively used e-business technologies to assemble a complementing offering for aftermarket services. The customers are supplied with online (visual) documentation, repair manuals, diagnostics tools, and so on from Boeing and its major systems suppliers. These make it possible for customers to significantly streamline maintenance and service operations because they can greatly simplify the complex paper-based procedure to assure that the right instructions are used. The customized tools for spare parts management and supplier contacts complete the complementing offering from Boeing and its suppliers.

A similar value innovation has been made in the PC business. One of the characteristics of this business is the high frequency of hardware and software problems, or at least a multitude of unexpected problem situations. Toshiba is one of the companies to build online help desks to reduce the pain among customers. Besides the basic functionality, the customers are provided with technically advanced software tools, such as online lessons-learnt databases. However, these lessons-learnt databases are typically offered by chat program suppliers, such as Ichat, just to name one. The more advanced these become, the more important the experience of other users becomes to the customer. The value innovation here is to bring in the experience and expertise of other users as part of the complementing offering.

Another point with complementing offerings is that introducing a third party into the customer-supplier relationship can catalyze value innovation. The experience of many manufacturing companies in their aftermarket services shows that a breakthrough between the customer and the supplier can be inhibited by a lack of logistics competencies.

In this situation, a coevolutionary breakthrough may just require the involvement of a third party. For example, a company designing and building large chemical plants contracted Caterpillar to manage its entire spare-parts business, because it was just not used to nonproject sales. That is, if we cannot find a win-win solution between the customer and the supplier we might succeed with a "win-win-win" scheme. The end customer benefits are created by a collaborative bundle of goods and services provided by the manufacturer and a logistics service provider. It is not only the customer that benefits but also the manufacturer and the service provider.

The overseas customers of DHL Europe illustrate how logistics service providers have enabled value innovation. Original equipment manufacturers face serious challenges in setting up aftermarket services in Europe. Typical problems are very slow inventory turnover time (from months to even years) and customers dissatisfied with the level of service support in their national language. And companies such as Kubota (tractors etc.), Focus (overhead beamers), and Harley-Davidson (motorbikes) have the additional challenge of replenishing their spare-parts inventories from overseas. This longer replenishment lead time quickly drives up the inventory investment needed to supply the European aftermarket customers with a high level of service.

The solution offered to the Japanese and American manufacturers, among others, was a spare-parts inventory service center located in the proximity of the DHL European hub. The hub itself has a central location in Europe, being

---

SUBSTITUTING INVENTORY WITH INFORMATION

Inventory carrying cost elements quickly sum up to a high proportion of the total inventory value. We can arrive at a rough estimate of the annual inventory holding costs for the PC business by summing up the capital costs (10 percent) and the price erosion (25 percent), which equal 35 percent of the value of the inventory. An excellent rule of thumb is then reached by calculating the inventory carrying cost for each 10 days: $10d \times 35\%/365 = 1\%$. So, the reduction or increase of 10 days of supply (DOS) in inventory has an impact of 1 percent on the return on sales.

Using this rule of thumb, we see that the profitability advantage of Dell over Compaq due to different levels of inventories (10 DOS vs. 40 DOS) is 3 percent in the return on sales. This difference can basically be leveraged as:

➤ Higher profitability for the supplier.

➤ Lower prices for the end consumer.

➤ Both lower prices for the consumer and a higher return for the supplier.

What has this to do with value innovation? The point is that the days of supply in the supply chain are best reduced by collaboration. Customers can receive lower prices if they purchase direct from the manufacturer and are prepared to wait a few days while the computer is built. But, for customers to change the way they purchase, the supplier needs to be reliable in addition to fast and inexpensive.

part of the Zaventem international airport complex just outside Brussels, the capital of the European Union. Urgent spare-parts requirements from anywhere in Europe can be fulfilled in just 24 hours by using the standard logistics services of DHL. And, replenishment lead times from overseas can also be significantly reduced by using air freight.

The improved service levels have extraordinary impact on the sales organizations and aftersales partners for these American and Japanese manufacturers. As the service level from the hub can be assured, local spare-parts inventories become redundant. Having a single stock-keeping point, and transparent demand, for all of Europe also provides a major inventory-carrying reduction for the distant manufacturers.

■ TAKING A NEW PERSPECTIVE ON COSTS

The second viewpoint for unraveling value innovation in the demand-supply chain is cost. Taking a new perspective on cost is key for understanding many value innovations. The pioneering collaborative business processes that we see today stem from companies taking a different perspective on costs and their trade-offs. Maybe the best known is a slogan from Dell: "Substituting inventory with information." However, there are many other possibilities for approaching value innovation from a cost perspective. In the following subsections, we explore cost and efficiency from two different angles and point out their potential to serve as the platform for value innovation:

1. Collaborate to manage price erosion.
2. Collaborate to reduce interaction costs.

➤ Collaborate to Manage Price Erosion

Price erosion and risk are major problems in industries where fashion and technological innovation drive a rapid introduction of new products to the market. For many companies, inventory holding costs have been the eye-opener leading to value innovations (i.e., a new offering that provides customers with a quantum increase in value). Inventory holding costs are composed of:

➤ Obsolescence (i.e., price erosion, scrap, deterioration).
➤ Lost sales.
➤ Personnel costs (inventory related labor).
➤ Fixed assets (space, equipment).
➤ Insurance.
➤ Administration (stock keeping, IT costs, etc.).
➤ Capital costs (for raw materials, finished goods, work-in-progress).

Channel customers, like wholesalers and retailers, try to protect themselves by demanding that suppliers provide price protection clauses. However, price protection is a blunt instrument. Price erosion is a consequence of the learning curve in manufacturing and product development. When a particular product comes in fashion, or a new technology becomes available, many suppliers are able to quickly introduce the new product to the market and price erosion for older products is unstoppable. Instead of offering customers price protection, innovative suppliers have found that the way out is to try to shift focus and prevent inventories from building up.

The value innovation opportunity is to develop collaborative demand-supply chain management methods such as channel inventory visibility, shorter order fulfillment lead times, and advanced, collaborative replenishment methods to reduce the impact of price erosion for all the parties in the demand-supply chain including producers and trade customers.

The PC business is a well-known example of price erosion. However, there are similar examples of price erosion in industry after industry where fashion and technology drive new product development.

In the computer and telecommunication industries, the magnitude of price erosion has been in the range of 20 to 30 percent a year. In the mobile phone business, one of the best ever selling analog cellular phones was Nokia 121, whose street price in Finland at the launching phase in February 1992 was roughly USD 1500. As the product was ramped down October 1995 (i.e., 3½ years after launch), the street price had declined to the level of USD 250. The nominal annual price erosion was 24 percent.

In the PC business, price erosion has been even higher than in mobile phones. Memory chips, for example, experienced annual price erosion of 80 percent during the last years of the 1990s. This trend was only interrupted by an earthquake in Taiwan, which is one of the main regions supplying this technology.

Price erosion is at least as critical from the customer's viewpoint as from the supplier's view. Imagine a retail customer that has inventories full of products that are made obsolete by a new product introduction. Such events are common in the PC supply chain, where the launch of a new processor family from Intel instantly renders the previous generation hardware outdated.

No matter how big a breakthrough a value innovation is, one has always to bear in mind that unless it is built on innovations and process improvements, it is only temporary in nature. Dell Computer has been followed by many entrepreneurs imitating its direct business model. Even the players of the conventional channel are forcefully applying the same approaches, although the channel conflict has been a major obstacle slowing down their efforts. Because value innovation can build on learning from the customer relationship, however, a leading company, such as Dell, may continuously be able to "re-innovate" its business model. The result is that it is very difficult for a competitor to upstage the incumbents in a coevolutionary relationship.

➤ Collaborate to Reduce Interaction Costs

Another avenue toward value innovations is to look at interaction costs: What does the relationship cost the way it is set up at the moment?

Most relationships today are still built around orders, but as already pointed out, order-less relationships can many times be much more effective. The principle is that better information, such as inventory positions and forecasts, make it possible to reduce inventories while improving service levels.

One of the first examples of an order-less business model is Barilla, an Italian grocery manufacturer that in the late 1980s decided to apply just-in-time to grocery distribution. Barilla was able to drastically reduce the level of channel inventories by implementing vendor managed inventory (VMI) with key customers. The key was proving to customers that getting rid of purchase ordering would not lead to higher interaction cost; on the contrary, interaction would be much more efficient through higher service levels and less obsolescence. This is possible through better quality information—the supplier is relieved from speculative forecasting-driven production surges. Instead, a supplier may produce against a more level customer demand signal.

In the case of Dell Computer, the interaction cost dimension is put in a larger perspective. Comparing an indirect channel to Dell's direct channel model, the difference in the total cost equation is paramount. An indirect channel consists of a manufacturer, a distributor, a retailer, and a consumer. A manufacturer produces the PC configuration and ships it to the distributor. The distributor first receives the product package from the manufacturer. Thereafter, he stores, and distributes the package to a retailer where it is to be sold from the retailer's stocks. The retailer's salesperson negotiates with the consumer, and if she is lucky enough to get the deal, she produces the sales documents and bills the consumer. The consumer needs to take a sequence of several intermittent actions before having the product in use. First he has to get to a point-of-sales (POS), negotiate, and make the deal with the retailer. Then he has to have the purchase transferred from POS to the point-of-use (POU). The total interaction costs when also considering the time and effort spent by the consumer to search and shop around before completing a sale can be several hundred dollars.

For a customer who values time, there is a place for value innovations. By tailoring offerings to corporate customers, a company such as Dell can radically reduce interaction costs. It is not only the purchasing process that can be made convenient, it is also the installation and aftersales support.

The customer-supplier relationship can incorporate numerous sources of inefficiencies. The elimination or bypassing of these can lead to value innovations. The supplier and customer being on different continents is one such source of inefficiency. The following example with a third-party solutions provider illustrates this opportunity.

As mentioned, outsourcing, such as using a logistics service provider, can catalyze value innovation. This is also the case for a manufacturer exporting to the Asia-Pacific region. Asia-Pacific is a region where domestic industries have been protected by governmental regulations, such as import taxes and customs fees. Therefore, it is not at all obvious whether a European or American manufacturer should export an assembled product or just the components for local final value-adding operations. The cost difference can be 20 to 30 percent, in the form of import tax. On the other hand, it always is a major investment for a producer to launch a local manufacturing operation.

If the complexity of a value-adding operation, like final configuration and assembly, is small, the producer can outsource final configuration to the trade customer or someone partnering with him. Inside a common market, like the European Union, there is no need for such arrangements but in regions with barriers between the countries, such as the Asia-Pacific region, simply outsourcing final assembly to the channel partner can be a value innovation. Also, an express courier with inventory facilities (e.g., DHL, FedEX, UPS) could also be used by smaller exporters to gain access to local distribution and retail channels.

■ EXTENDING DELIVERY TO FULFILLMENT

The final perspective on value innovation in the demand-supply chain is extending delivery to fulfillment. This means that there are opportunities to value innovation in how the delivery is made, and in adjusting that to how the customer uses the product after the delivery. This section covers three issues:

1. Expeditious, convenient delivery.
2. Digital distribution of goods and services.
3. Synchronized operations with the customer.

➤ Expeditious, Convenient Delivery

Sometimes the cost aspect is not the primary reason for customers to change the way they operate. This is the case when the value offering has clear immediate advantages. Expeditious, convenient delivery can be such a value innovation.

For example, the one-hour photo development service we touched on earlier may sound trivial, but it revolutionized the photo distribution business. Fast-response photo shops penetrated the markets in the early 1980s. The basic idea of a one-hour photo service is brilliantly simple.

Before launching this business model, the customers had to wait for several days to get exposures developed and hard copies produced. In the 1970s the lead time was even longer. One week was not unusual. The long lead time was very much due to the economies of scale sought in film processing. In the 1980s, however, new solutions became available that made it possible to efficiently develop prints at the point-of-sale. Before long, the investment costs were low enough to bring the one-hour service also to small street corner photo shops. The quantum improvement in value for the consumers was clearly linked to the speed of delivery and the wide availability of the service in everyday shopping centers. But it was not the speed as such, but the convenience. The consumers could drop off their films for processing when they arrived at the mall. The films were then developed and the prints produced while the customer was shopping. When leaving the mall, the customer could pick up the prints. It eliminated extra visits or having to remember to get the prints.

From the supplier's point of view, the model is attractive because, once established in a good location, it is possible to build up a customer base that is willing to pay for fast and convenient delivery. For price-sensitive customers, there still is the alternative—using centralized photo processing laboratories. No price premiums for convenience exist, but the supplier can balance capacity with demand to cut costs.

It is interesting to consider one-hour photo shops from the viewpoint of interactions. At the first glance, it may appear that the one-hour photo shop is definitely more cost-efficient compared with the traditional model, where the processing factory and the photo shop are two separate institutions (see Figure 3.2). However, what is easy to forget is the scale aspect. In the one-hour model, each point-of-sale must invest in processing facilities.

Hou Lee, a Stanford University professor, and the director of the Global Supply Chain Management Forum at Stanford University would call such a production arrangement postponed manufacturing. The postponement is achieved by investing in hardware at the point-of-sales (POS). The eliminating of the processing factory is offset by investment in the point-of-sales. Additionally, due to the different scale

A. Traditional photo business model

Photo factory   Photo shop   Consumer

B. One-hour photo business model

Desktop factory and
photo shop   Consumer

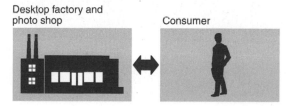

Figure 3.2 The Traditional Photo Business Model versus One-Hour Photo Shop Concept

in the POS (maybe only ten consumers a day) compared with the scale in a photo factory (thousands to tens of thousands consumers a day), the unit costs per film produced is significantly smaller in the traditional business model. However, this is offset by creating a more stable relationship through fast delivery at a location where the consumer has to spend time anyway.

➤ Digital Distribution of Goods and Services

What will come next in the photo industry remains to be seen. But as digital cameras are getting more and more advanced in their technological features and consumer prices fall, we may be facing a new discontinuity in the business.

This takes us to the topic of value innovations and digital distribution of goods and services. In the analog, plastic film based supply chain, much of the business was based on variable costs. The consumers bought films that were exposed, developed, and made into prints. With digital technology, the consumable film is replaced by reusable semiconductor memories and only those exposures that the customer explicitly wants a hard copy of are developed.

The new entrants in the field are companies such as Sony and Hewlett-Packard that are not burdened by the logic of the physical supply chain for film and processing. Increasingly, consumer electronics retailers rather than photo shops distribute photo equipment. Sony already provides a complete service solution for any photographer keen on slides. And Hewlett-Packard, one of the leaders in printer technology, has a new solution for those photographers who want to stick to prints.

The photo example demonstrates how technological innovation opens up new opportunities for value innovation and makes some previously great models obsolete. It is important to notice that technological innovation does not automatically lead to value innovations.

Digital distribution of goods and services makes new offerings possible that completely change the way the customer and supplier work together. In the current situation where only the leading edge companies have fully leveraged the opportunities for effective product/service delivery, there are ample opportunities for value innovation with digital distribution of goods and services.

What has digital distribution meant for the software supply chain? Shareware distributors exploited the possibility more than a decade ago, and today Internet software retailers, such as Buydirect and Download have built their supply chain entirely on digital distribution.

F-Secure, one of the leading virus protection companies in the world uses a more advanced solution. The company was the first to introduce security products for wireless communications, transactions, and e-commerce. However, it has also been a value innovator with its "Security and Service" offering. The value innovation is to provide the customer with a timely stream of software upgrades, to protect the customer from loss and inconvenience caused by virus attacks. Each time an employee in the customer company logs on to the company intranet, his or her computer is automatically updated with the latest version of the virus protection software. The virus protection business is faced with new challenges on a daily basis, and new releases need to be distributed expediently. Without digital distribution, tens of software releases per annum for millions of workstations would be an impossible task for both the software company logistics and the customer companies' help desks.

Another opportunity for value innovation is to apply the logic of software upgrades to physical products. Here, digital distribution is the basis for a customer relationship where the product is improved as the requirements of the customer evolve. Imagine a student purchasing a basic vacuum cleaner for his dormitory residence—at the basic level price. Later, when moving into a house of his own, he could upgrade the vacuum cleaner with autopilot for an additional charge. Such a scenario is not simply a fiction. Television sets and VCRs are examples of products where prototypes already exist applying this logic.

Maybe the most advanced forms of digital distribution have been created by the companies in cellular telecommunication.

Their distribution systems don't even need cabling—neither for power nor for data. Nokia has developed a system for over-the-air software upgrades for their high-end cellular phones. These upgrades can drastically change the functionality of the physical product (e.g., Nokia's mobile Communicator). The technology applied is called short messaging (SMS). Interestingly, SMS is just a standard messaging protocol, normally used as an inexpensive media to transmit simple text messages between two cellular phone users. Nokia has leveraged this technology and created the means for developing new value innovations to link itself closer to its customers.

➤ Synchronized Operations with the Customer

In the networked business models, the supplier can also add value to the customer by integrating the delivery with the customer's business processes. The opportunity for value innovation is in the fulfillment of the customer's goals; for example, to increase retail category sales or reduce production costs, not just to deliver products.

Developments in collaborative planning, forecasting, and replenishment (CPFR) indicate the opportunities. The best known example of CPFR is that of Wal-Mart with Procter & Gamble in the early 1990s. The culmination point of this joint development was the CFAR (See Far) collaborative planning system set up for maximizing sales and minimizing waste and inefficiency.

Inspired by the example of Wal-Mart's and P&G's collaboration, others have followed suit and started experimenting with new collaborative business processes. A more recent example of a collaborative forecasting, planning, and replenishment program has been reported by Heineken in the United States. In the Heineken case, the suppliers report inventory levels and adjust their forecasts online on the Heineken Web site, thereby ensuring high availability and service for themselves, but also providing Heineken with the most up-to-date demand information to plan production and distribution.

Synchronizing deliveries to the customer operation can also be a value innovation. Plastal is a Scandinavian plastics company that, among other things, supplies bumpers to the automobile industry. In the convertible segment, where Porsche and Saab are the key brands that Plastal supplies, Valmet Automotives is the contract manufacturer assembling the convertibles. The production scheduling at the assembly plant is customer order driven. This means that the assembly sequence can be practically any mix of the models and variants assembled in the plant.

From the viewpoint of the bumper supplier, the assembly plant also reserves the right to change the production plan on short notice due to the changes in their order book, material availability, or the like. The upstream partner, Plastal, is informed about the assembly sequence three hours prior the first operation in the assembly line. An extra challenge is the physical dimensions of the bumpers. They take up a lot of space and are easily damaged, in particular after the painting process.

In the early 1990s, Plastal experimented with different kinds of buffering systems to satisfy the customer's delivery requirements. Gradually, they realized that due to the sheer number of variants and low production volumes, predicting demand for a specific variant was impossible. Some of the color and feature combinations would always become obsolete due to short production series, while there would also be color and feature combinations that were always out of stock.

In this situation, Plastal reconsidered their delivery service philosophy. The resulting value innovation was to deliver directly to the point-of-use in the assembly. The shipping schedule was first synchronized with the customer's production schedule—the sequence of the bumpers shipped from the supplier (Plastal) followed exactly the sequence of the cars assembled in the plant (Valmet) with lot size of one. Next, Plastal also synchronized the production with the assembly plant. Instead of batch production, a call-off message (for a particular bumper configuration for a particular car to be assembled) triggers the production of the particular bumper, one by one.

There is no finished bumper inventory at Plastal. For cost-efficiency reasons, the bumpers are shipped in batches to the customer and forwarded in the manufactured sequence to the customer's point-of-use. As there is a nonzero risk of quality defects of bumpers, the customer does have a buffer (one per configuration) of ready-made bumpers in the close proximity of the assembly line. Figure 3.3 illustrates the operation before and after synchronization. As a result of the closer collaboration, Plastal has been able not only to improve the value to the customer by a quantum leap, but also to improve cost efficiency in its own operation.

■ COEVOLUTION—BEWARE OF THE TRAPS!

The challenge for demand-supply chain management is building the right kind of positive feedback loops. The problem is that collaboration and being a commodity supplier are two sides of the same coin. It is important to understand that a coevolutionary process not only can increase the value added, but also can destroy it.

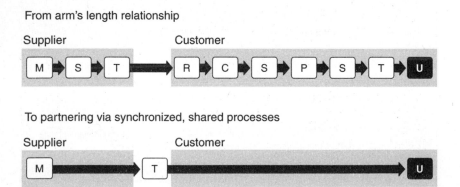

Figure 3.3 The Solution for Synchronizing by the Bumper Supplier (Plastal) with the Porsche and Saab Convertible Car Production in the Assembly Plant (Notation: M: make; R: receive; C: check; S: store; P: pick; T: transport; U: use)

DELL COMPUTER CORPORATION

As Michael Dell started to assemble customized PCs from his dormitory at the University of Texas, Austin, it was the beginning of a business model that would reshape not only the computer business, but also industrial practices. What he did was to focus the whole business—not just sales—on the end customer with an ingeniously simple business idea: sell one—buy one—make one—distribute one! This simple business model stands in stark contrast to the mainstream mass production model of buy one—make one—distribute one—sell one (sometimes with the last step "scrap one," as a customer could not always be found).

It is no coincidence that Dell Computer reached the number two position in the PC business globally in the late 1990s, and the number one position in the United States in October 1999. The build-to-order concept has several advantages that can be used for value innovations (i.e., improving the customer's operations and performance by changing the value offering).

A value offering is not a single-faceted issue. There are manifold reasons for the success of Dell's value offerings. The value offerings changed the customers' purchasing behavior to favor Dell by:

➤ Reshaping the customer relationship.
➤ Taking a new perspective on costs.
➤ Extending delivery to fulfillment.

The offering Dell makes today is to provide the customer with exactly the right product configuration. Therefore the most obvious route to understand what Dell is doing is to focus on how Dell manages the customer relationship. Dell allowed—in fact, insisted—that the customer specify the desired configuration. And, even though in the Dell model, capital is not tied in inventories and the obsolescence risk is minimal, the market growth of Dell could never have been realized without an offering that changed corporate customers' purchasing processes. This was the first value innovation.

(continued)

DELL COMPUTER CORPORATION (CONTINUED)

In addition, Dell was able to turn the apparent handicap of no distribution channel into a virtue. By focusing on large corporate customers, the lack of local points of sales could actually be turned into an advantage. A large corporation with geographically dispersed locations found in Dell a supplier that could help the corporation coordinate and standardize its PC purchases. Dell has succeeded in addressing the requirements of large corporations, with essentially only a key account organization.

Dealing directly with corporate customers created an additional benefit, the opportunity to keep costs down, while volume and market shares grew. Mass distribution channels would have provided access to mass markets but the drawback would have been increased cost in the form of product obsolescence, markups, and transaction costs in the channel. As Dell grew, the scale advantages inherent in the direct model also created an effective buffer against lower margins. By having a minimum amount of inventories in the pipeline (i.e., minimizing the inventory carrying costs), the company is able to improve the return on sales.

By working together with its customers, Dell's account managers have been able to learn about the headaches of the corporate IT managers firsthand. This has further shifted the attention from product delivery to fulfillment. Dell gradually became aware that sourcing new PC hardware was among the easiest tasks of IT managers, but managing the desktops and software of users was not. By working with customers, key account managers learned about the whole spectrum of help desk tasks, how difficult it is to maintain software and hardware standards, and plan the roll out of new corporatewide standards for all users. With these insights, the key account managers were able to provide valuable help in these difficult areas.

Early on, the Internet was identified as a platform to provide all customers, not just corporate customers, with a full range of support services, ranging from hardware configuration to the IT help desk. It is not surprising that this has had an impact on both corporate IT management and end user support.

DELL COMPUTER CORPORATION (CONTINUED)

A third value innovation at Dell builds on the previous:

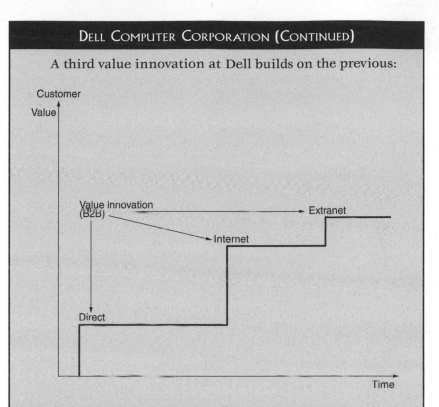

Three Value Innovations in Dell Computer's Corporate Sales

By offering corporate customers the ability to tailor their purchasing process, and relationship with the company, Dell is becoming an integral part of its customers' business processes. Actually, Dell is offering the business process to the customer by launching extranet sites that deal with PC-related issues for all the customer's employees. The beauty of this solution is self-service—once set up, the customer himself integrates with Dell step-by-step. In the end, sites literally speak the language of the customer, are cobranded by the customer, and provide solutions typically encountered with the particular customer. Dell has dedicated sites for each major customer that has accepted the offer for such a service. The customer's employees might not even recognize that it actually is not their site but a customized site provided by one of their IT suppliers.

To illustrate the implications of coevolution, consider the following example. Exhaustingly long working hours put in by junior staff within an organization may be the result of the coevolution between an organization's preference for staff that shows commitment and the staff's dependence on putting in long hours for career success. It is a typical positive feedback situation. The organization rewards staff that show commitment by making that extra effort, and members of the staff notice that a quick way to succeed is to put in extra hours and effort. Both seem to win in the short term: The organization can identify and reward committed junior staff, and junior staff—ready to put in the extra effort—progress in their careers. But, there is a downside. The company is soon trapped in a situation where the ever longer working hours restrict its opportunities to hire, or keep, young people who want also to succeed in other areas than work.

We bring this up because you need to be aware of the dangers of coevolutionary "blind alleys" or "competitive traps." Three common situations are:

1. Commodity trap.
2. Service trap.
3. Express-delivery trap.

➤ Commodity Trap

Academics and consultants have recently criticized Wal-Mart's and P&G's collaborative business model. This criticism is not so much due to the collaborative model itself but to its dynamics, or rather the lack of dynamics. Since the model was developed, P&G's brands have been bypassed by the customers' in-house brand. Despite setting up a collaborative business process, P&G fell into the commodity trap.

A commodity trap is a situation where the customers consider the supplier's products and service to simply be one alternative in a range of other equally good substitutes. The result is that the customer can make the supplier compete for business by lowering price. To stay competitive, the supplier must be able to offer an even lower price the next time around, until it is not possible to go any lower. Just as the peacock's tail cannot get any bigger and flashier, the prices in a commodity business also cannot go any lower. The primary selection criterion is low price—thus leaving the supplier with just barely enough margin to survive.

The commodity trap can be avoided, even by suppliers of commodity products. An excellent example is Würth, a supplier of nuts and bolts that will be discussed in Chapter 4. In Finland, Würth has leveraged its original equipment manufacturer customer's demand chains and come up with a mix of value-adding services for the customer's production, plant maintenance, and aftermarket operations. Würth's business model has been received with enthusiasm among its customers. This enthusiasm has been capitalized in the form of increased revenue and market share, indicating that the company has been able to escape the commodity trap.

➤ **Service Trap**

But giving customers the service they ask for can also trap a supplier company. In the service trap, the supplier gives the customers everything that is required, up to and beyond the supplier's capabilities and the cost and benefit justifications.

To avoid falling in the service trap, the first rule of thumb is to never promise more than what can be done within the capabilities on hand. A simple way to ensure this is the packaging of both services and products. For example, IBM Global Services has tried to treat services as SKUs (stock-keeping units). With this logic, a service that cannot be delivered is out of stock. The trick is essentially that you avoid the service trap by standardizing your service.

In the mid-1990s, the European mobile phone industry was reaching the fast growth section on the growth S-curve. At the time, a large consumer electronics company was poised to challenge and catch up with the market leaders. However, the leaders already had a big competitive advantage and a strong influence in the distribution channels.

The consumer electronics company saw its opportunity in providing better service to the end customer. Because mobile phones at the time had high field failure rates, the company thought a swap program would be a certain success with the consumer. So, as part of its quest for increased revenue and market share, the company decided to offer a 24-hour swap program for end customers. In practice, this value offering meant that the customer with a broken mobile phone was guaranteed a free new or repaired phone within 24 hours from the customer's claim.

The results from the challenger's point of view were not what had been hoped for. First of all, the reverse logistics process required to handle a swap program are not very straightforward and are far from inexpensive. A customer with a broken phone had to be reached wherever she happened to be on the globe. It did not matter whether the customer was skiing in the Alps, or hiking in Lapland, the service was to provide that customer with a replacement phone.

It turned out to be a highly labor-intensive process for the third-party logistics service providers to manage the material flows both from the consumers to the supplier and from the supplier to the consumers. Another critical element was the effect on consumer behavior. Field failure rates suddenly multiplied because customers started to return their phones even for minor technical or performance problems.

➤ Express-Delivery Trap

In business-to-consumer e-commerce, many start-up companies are prepared to invest heavily to reach a 24-hour order fulfillment lead time and a service level close to 100 percent. For example Webvan, an e-grocery company, decided up front to invest one billion dollars in a network of automated warehouses. This warehouse network serves as picking and distribution centers for consumer orders of groceries.

In January 2000, the business news reported that the stock value of eToys—an Internet retailer—suddenly fell by 20 percent. The reason was the investors' reaction to the news that eToys was to invest in new distribution facilities. Management had become frustrated with the third-party logistics service providers and as a response eToys was to own and run the key elements of the distribution system, including warehouses.

Why this concern? The third-party logistics providers could only achieve 96 percent on-time-delivery performance given the 24-hour order fulfillment lead-time promise. From an outsider's perspective, 96 percent looks quite decent, but the management of eToys used Amazon's 99 percent as the benchmark.

Put another way, the e-tailers appear to have been caught in an express-delivery trap. Some of the players inside the e-business community have started to talk about f-business instead of e-business emphasizing that it is the fulfillment that will make the difference among the e-business companies. The issue is seen as: "Anyone can sell a book on the Internet, but how many can deliver it expeditiously at low cost to the consumer?"

Not all companies fall into this trap when going on the Internet. On the business-to-business side, Cisco orchestrates a network where the customers on one hand and the suppliers on the other receive online information about the delivery capabilities throughout the chain. Dell Computer, our example from the computer industry, is segmenting their services depending on the customer's profile. However, the company never promises a delivery shorter than their build-to-order capability.

■ VALUE INNOVATION AND DEMAND-SUPPLY CHAIN CONFIGURATION

Recognizing the value that makes a difference can catalyze a fast development of new business solutions (value innovation to reshape the demand-supply chain).

You can approach value innovation from three basic directions: reshaping the customer relationship, acquiring a new perspective on costs, and extending delivery to fulfillment. Value innovations in the customer relationship can increase the convenience of buying, the degree of personalization, and the range of complementary offerings. Looking at costs collaboration changes the perspective. Through collaboration, the price erosion in fashion and high-tech industries can be managed; collaborative offerings also are key to reduce interaction costs. Expanding delivery to fulfillment opens up opportunities for innovations in how and when the delivery is made.

The supplier can speed up the value innovation process, but the process is coevolutionary and it can only be reached by collaborating with customers. Varied terms and conditions support value innovation. The newly developed e-business technologies and e-business related collaborative models seem to open a vast spectrum of opportunity for value innovation that is still unexplored and not yet exploited.

The best way to start the coevolutionary process of value innovation is to make a new value offering that "locks the customer on." When customers experience the benefits the supplier offers, customer lock-on to the particular supplier is created.

However, suppliers need to be aware that there is another aspect to coevolution. There are real risks in making the wrong offer. Such an offer can start a runaway development where the supplier ends up with no, or very thin margins. Besides the commodity trap, there are the service and delivery traps where the supplier may end up meeting performance levels that customers really do not employ for anything, but simply use for choosing among competing suppliers.

Chapter 4 focuses on how to make it all happen. We discuss how to use the value offering point (VOP) and the order penetration point (OPP) to find new value innovations. Mastering these tools is a basic management skill for value innovation in the demand-supply chain.

■ REFERENCE

1. W. Chan Kim and Reneé Mauborgne, "Strategy, Value Innovation, and the Knowledge Economy," *Sloan Management Review,* Spring 1999, 41–54.

Chapter

Reshaping Your Value Offering—How to Do It

The order penetration point (OPP) and value offering point (VOP) are your tools to reshape your demand-supply chain. How do you successfully collaborate with your customers in practice and leverage customer relationships to improve your own efficiency? How do you make adjustments in the supply chain that also improve your customers' performance—their sales efficiency, transaction costs, and service to their customers?

This is tricky. Most of the changes suppliers make don't add much value from the customer's point of view. A typical fix for a supplier is to reduce inventory by reducing product variety, not much value for the customer's customer. Similarly, when you make or assemble to order the same products you used to deliver from stock, it is difficult to make the benefits of customization attractive enough to compensate for the longer delivery time. By understanding how the demand-supply chain works, however, it is possible to design supply chain innovations for different customers that will benefit both parties.

■ THE DEMAND-SUPPLY CHAIN

➤ The Supply Chain

A supply chain creates products and services that are transferred from suppliers to consumers (e.g., organizations, businesses, and private citizens). The supply chain for perishable packaged consumer goods would consist of manufacturing, packaging, distribution, and retailing. On the other hand, a supply chain for an original equipment manufacturer (OEM) could be configured as component manufacturing, assembly, distribution, and installation. Installation, rather than retailing is the last step in the supply chain, for example, for a supplier of elevators because the supplier can deal directly with the building contractor, bypassing intermediaries.

The supply chain for a manufacturer's main product line and for aftersales services are often different. A possible configuration for an elevator spare-parts supply chain is component manufacturing, warehousing, distribution, and installation. The same company often needs to operate several supply chains depending on customer demand. In the elevator example, the manufacturer needs different supply chains to satisfy demand for new elevators, as well as the demand to keep elevators in use.

The activities in the supply chain vary depending on the product and the type of demand. However, we can define a set of generic value-adding activities for the supply chain. These are "make" (e.g., manufacturing of materials or components), "combine" (e.g., assembly, packaging), "move" (e.g., distribution, collection), "store" (e.g., warehousing, retailing), and "customize" (e.g., installation, configuration). Delivery does not appear in the set of generic value-adding activities because delivery depends on the value offering. For order-less fulfillment models, the delivery can just as well be storing the product as moving it into customer premises.

Today, due to both new technology and business process innovations, we are starting to see these generic supply chain activities in new guises, sequences, and combinations: Supply chain reconfiguration is becoming more commonplace. In a bricks-and-mortar retail store, the customer herself usually takes the product with her home after she has made the purchase. The last step of the supply chain is displaying the product on the shelves—the last step is to store the product, not to move it. Today, however, physical display of the product is not important in the business-to-consumer setup; instead to moving the product (delivering the product to the consumer) is the critical last step of the supply chain. Also, customization activities are increasingly being added to different locations in the supply chain. The product may be configured in connection with the physical assembly or packaging of the product (customize in assembly) or on the way to the end customer (customize on the move), instead of at the time of delivery, or in aftersales.

➤ The Demand Chain

The demand chain transfers demand from markets to suppliers. A retailer's demand chain to a grocery supplier consists of assortment planning (deciding what to sell), inventory management (deciding the quantity of supplies needed), and the actual purchasing (see Figure 4.1).

The demand chain from a building contractor to an elevator manufacturer starts with the requirements for the new building (e.g., How many people will work there? How quickly do they need to get in and out?). The next step is the architect's blueprints of the building, followed by the project plan and timetable, and finally supplier selection and purchasing.

Just as a supplier may have many different supply chains to manage, a supplier's customer may have distinct demand chains that you can analyze one-by-one. The demand chain

Assortment planning	Inventory management	Purchasing
Decide what to sell	Decide how much is needed	Decide where to acquire what is needed

Figure 4.1 Retailer's Demand Chain

for a new elevator is distinctly different from the demand chain for elevator spare parts. In the aftersales demand chain, the key activity is maintenance planning, followed by parts requirements, possibly also inventory management, and finally purchasing.

The demand chain translates a customer objective into information that the supplier can act on; it is a decision-making process. The four generic decision-making steps of the customer demand chain are:

1. Define purpose (e.g., retail in consumer goods, rent out office building).
2. Plan (e.g., category plan, blueprint for office building).
3. Manage consumption and requirements (e.g., inventory management, project management).
4. Purchase transaction (e.g., replenishment order, purchase order).

The customer really does not need to make all decisions himself to realize an objective. For example, a contractor responsible for building an office building can invite a number of elevator suppliers to present their solutions for moving people efficiently and safely in the new office building. After evaluating their proposals, the contractor selects one solution, and lets the selected supplier make the project management and ordering decisions for installing the elevators on his own. In the same way, a retailer may, based on a category plan, decide that for gift cards and other paper products a specific supplier can deliver better results if allowed to take full responsibility for the day-to-day management of requirements and supply.

➤ The Demand-Supply Chain

Working together, the demand and supply chains create the demand-supply chain. When the two chains work well together, we say that supply is well synchronized with demand, or that the supplier provides customers with value added services.

The most basic example of demand and supply chains working together is a wholesaler ordering goods from a packaged consumer goods manufacturer. When the order arrives, the manufacturer delivers the ordered goods to the wholesaler's warehouse from his own warehouse or production line. Here the wholesaler calls all the shots in the demand chain; the wholesaler plans the assortment, manages inventory, and makes the purchase decision that triggers a delivery. Also, the supplier only provides the product as specified by the wholesaler's purchase order.

But there is no reason why the packaged consumer goods supplier could not be active in the demand chain. For example, the supplier could be responsible for the availability of goods in the wholesaler's inventory, and make decisions on replenishment orders on behalf of the customer. In this case, the responsibility of the supplier extends further down the supply chain (to the wholesaler's warehousing) but also further back in the customer's demand chain (to the wholesaler's inventory management).

Herlitz, a European gift card and writing paper supplier that takes responsibility for a retailer's whole category is another example. To deliver the higher value added, the supplier takes care of managing the shelf in the retail store (an extension to the retail stage in the supply chain). At the same time, in the demand chain, Herlitz takes over responsibility for the assortment decisions within the category, inventory management, and replenishment orders. The retailer simply retains the decision in the demand chain on whether to keep the category or not in her retail stores, and which supplier to use to provide it.

How can we describe the interaction between the customer's demand chain and the supply chain? To explore ways for synchronizing supply with demand and for creating more value for the customer, it is essential to understand how the two chains are linked.

They are linked in two places—the order penetration point and the value offering point. By changing how demand is linked to supply, we can synchronize the supply chain better, and by changing the link from supply to demand, we can increase value added for the customer.

■ THE ORDER PENETRATION POINT (OPP) LINKS DEMAND TO SUPPLY

The *order penetration point* (OPP) is the point in the supply chain at which customer demand (an order) is allocated to the product (see Figure 4.2). The goods might be allocated from a warehouse once the order is received, or they might be manufactured to order. Each order penetration point has different costs and benefits for both the supplier and customer.

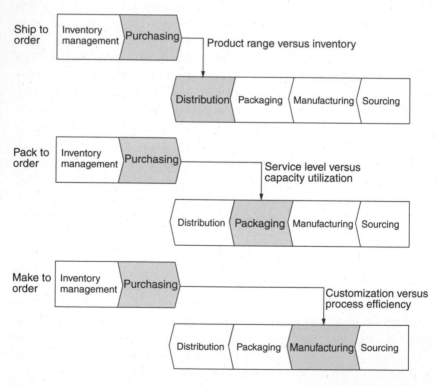

Figure 4.2 Moving the Order Penetration Point Changes the Supplier's Economics

If the order is allocated from the supplier's distribution center (and if the item is in stock), the supplier can assure rapid delivery. Rapid delivery (benefit for the customer) therefore depends on a large inventory (cost for the supplier). And, of course, the larger the product range, the larger the necessary inventory. So either the supplying company incurs large inventory costs to keep delivery time to a minimum, or it reduces inventory at the risk of not being able to quickly fulfill orders.

Moving the OPP back to packaging or assembly—the point at which goods are assembled into finished products (e.g., soap is poured into a cardboard box and sealed; components are assembled into a PC)—cuts down on inventory costs for the supplier. This is a huge cost benefit for the supplier, especially in situations where there is fast price erosion.

The customer, however, will have to wait longer for delivery, as the goods still have to be packaged or assembled once ordered. In the automotive industry, a customer that has ordered a popular model sometimes has to wait weeks, perhaps even months, before there is available capacity and his car is built. A solution for the supplier is to install more assembly capacity to bring the delay back down, but this is costly!

If the supplier does not want to keep the customer waiting, nor invest in extra assembly or packaging capacity, there is sometimes a solution through product and process design. This solution is to postpone as late as possible the process steps that create variants. Hewlett-Packard has successfully used this approach to deal with local variants of laser printers. The laser printers that are assembled are all identical, regardless of country-specific requirements, and the local variations are only made later in the country in which they will be sold. The OPP is postponed to the warehouse where a few critical assembly and packaging operations can still be performed to order. The benefit is that you can have a wider product range without increasing inventory, while avoiding the trade-off between longer delivery times and need to invest in capacity reserves. This is all very well, but moving assembly tasks to a distribution center involves another trade-off—postponement versus quality. It is difficult to perform complex process steps as reliably and efficiently in several distribution centers as in a single assembly plant.

Moving the OPP back yet further to manufacture-to-order makes it possible to meet individual customer specifications. But this comes at a high cost for the customer in terms of speed of delivery, while process efficiency declines for the supplier each time a standard design is abandoned in favor of a customized one.

The further the OPP is moved back upstream in the supply chain, the longer it takes to fulfill the order, but the more flexibility there is to configure the product. The advantage of this to the supplier will depend on the balance between cost savings and what the customer gains or has to forfeit. It is never a win-win situation in that the customer and supplier benefit equally. Moving the OPP point back in the supply chain reduces the risk that the supplier produces products that the customer does not want, but the customer may have to wait longer for the products that he wants.

Ship-to-order, assemble-to-order, and make-to-order are the basic alternatives for the order penetration point. But what if the customer does not place purchase orders? We could change the definition and start talking about "ship-to-demand" and so on. But for the supply chain, it does not really matter whether it is the customer, or the supplier that is responsible for order generation. This is also why we are content to stick with "order" to label the event that triggers supply. Instead, we will deal with the issue of "What is the demand?" by introducing a new mechanism—the value offering point.

■ THE VALUE OFFERING POINT (VOP) LINKS SUPPLY TO DEMAND

The value offering point (VOP) is the second point that links the demand and supply chains. It is the point in the customer's demand chain where the supplier fulfills demand. Moving the VOP largely benefits the customer, and requires the supplier to do more work. There are three major VOPs (see Figure 4.3).

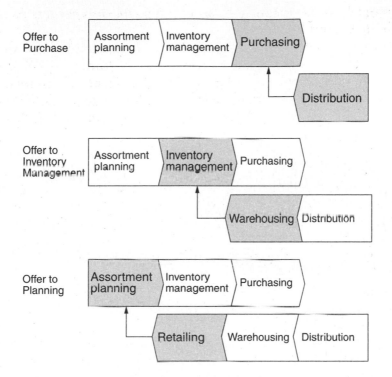

Figure 4.3 Three Major Value Offering Points

An offer to purchase is the conventional, arm's-length buyer/seller relationship, where the VOP is the customer's purchasing department. The purchasing department decides who supplies the goods needed, and when they are needed. The offer's competitiveness depends primarily on product range, price, and delivery accuracy and speed.

Here, e-commerce technology can significantly improve the offering. For example, commodity suppliers that collaborate through online procurement catalogs extend the product range of their offering with that of complementing suppliers. Purchasing aggregators and, at times also online marketplaces, enable the customer to reduce price. And, the online tracking services of logistics service providers support delivery accuracy. But the basic weakness of the conventional arm's-length relationship remains. Both the buyer and seller make independent decisions on how to deal with the risks of stockouts and obsolescence. The result is that periods of oversupply are followed by shortages as customers and suppliers struggle to optimize their own operations.

An offer to inventory management (i.e., taking over the customer's inventory management function) moves the VOP further back in the demand chain. By carefully monitoring the customer's inventory levels, the supplier can fulfill demand far more efficiently for the customer, helping reduce the cost to the customer of ordering stock that is never sold, and ensuring that the customer is never out of stock of those goods that are selling well. The trade-off for the supplier, however, is more work, as the supplier now has to have a separate inventory control process for each customer.

An offer to planning moves the VOP to merchandising (in the case of retailing), or production (as in the automotive and PC industries).

By collaborating on the assortment determination in retailing, for example, the supplier and retailer look together at consumer demand categories that the supplier's products serve. Through this, the supplier can avoid making new products or promotions that don't serve a purpose for the retailer. Suppliers are also expected to use this collaboration to improve their delivery performance. The result is more profitable use of retail space for the retailer. But unless the retailer can charge a premium for this kind of collaboration, the act of moving the VOP to merchandising has no automatic benefit for the supplier. The buying power of so many retailers today makes such a premium unlikely.

A fourth, and still largely unexplored VOP, is the offer to end user. Dell's direct sales model for business clients is one of the best-known examples. Rather than fulfilling orders from a wholesaler (an offer to purchase), Dell went all the way back in the demand chain to the end customer, offering to fulfill orders for customized PCs that could be delivered onto an employee's desk complete with the necessary software and configured for the network. All the user has to do is switch on. The enormous advantage to the corporate customer is that it can shut down half its PC support team, which spends much of its time setting up new computers.

Moving the VOP back in the demand chain reduces the risk that the customer does not get the necessary products to operate efficiently. Responding to demand earlier in the customer's decision-making process gives the supplier better information to act on, and more time to act.

■ WIN-WIN CONFIGURATIONS

Suppliers are already experimenting with both the OPP and the VOP to improve their supply chains. But how can a supplier find the solutions that will help increase customer value and supplier efficiency at the same time?

Moving the OPP can benefit both the supplier and customer, but neither benefits indisputably. Moving the OPP back in the supply chain will cut supplier costs, but increase the time needed to fulfill a customer's order. The supplier reduces the risk of producing the wrong products, but increases the risk of losing sales due to a slower response.

Moving the VOP is primarily to align the supplier with the customer's objectives, but this in turn also opens up opportunities for the supplier to increase sales. The opportunity is based on adapting to the customer, who is adapting to the supplier's value offering. In the process, customer functions begin to disappear and the supplier takes on new tasks and roles by providing value added services. In addition, the time available for the supplier to respond to customer demand also increases.

Time is the key to finding win-win configurations. Moving the OPP back in the supply chain increases the time needed to respond to customer demand, and moving the VOP increases the time available to respond. This means that, even though taking more responsibility for the customer operation requires more work from suppliers, they can benefit from moving the VOP if they simultaneously move the OPP. It is by understanding the interaction of both links in the chain that suppliers can optimize their supply chains to improve the customer's performance and make step changes in the efficiency of their own operations.

In the case of inventory management, a manufacturer might be keen to move the VOP back to inventory management to help the customer reduce lost sales and obsolescence costs. There will be high integration costs for the supplier, but by managing the customer's inventory, the supplier now has information about customer demand much earlier than would otherwise have been possible. This time advantage means the supplier can reduce its own inventory costs by packaging to order without the customer noticing any deterioration in delivery times. It is a win-win situation.

Likewise, competitors of Dell have difficulty profitably delivering such an excellent service to end users (can push the VOP back to the end customer) if they do not assemble to order as well. Dell receives customer demand information at an early stage in the demand chain making it possible to assemble to order without the customer objecting to the lead time.

And assembling to order makes value offerings to business end users, such as new employees, possible. In addition, Dell has eliminated inventory costs and, importantly, can now purchase components later than its competitors, when prices are lower. (How does assembling later to reach a customer, say, for Christmas, help Dell buy cheaper components? The simple answer is price erosion; the price of electronic components usually goes down over time.)

The development of Web applications has had a dramatic effect on implementing new demand chain solutions. With simple tools, a customer can publish daily inventory reports for its suppliers on the Web. Standard ERP package suppliers have also developed new functionality that enable suppliers to access prespecified reports over the Internet. These developments make it easier to set up collaborative demand chains, scale up solutions to a larger number of partners, and reduce the risk of getting locked in with a particular solution and partner.

■ HOW TO USE THE VOP AND OPP—FIVE BASIC STEPS

The VOP and OPP are practical tools to start working with demand and supply at the same time. You can start thinking

RECONFIGURING THE SUPPLY-DEMAND CHAIN— A NUTS AND BOLTS EXAMPLE

The Finnish company Würth Oy has delighted customers, improved its own efficiency, and earned itself a 40 percent price premium on the most everyday products—nuts and bolts—by reconfiguring its supply-demand chain.

This subsidiary of the German Würth Group, offers business customers products in fasteners and assembly technology products (nuts, bolts, screws, screwdrivers, etc.). Its 1998 sales worldwide were over 7 billion DM. In Finland, Würth Oy has a product range of 28,000 different items.

Demand for such products is generally driven by customers' maintenance, repair, and assembly operations. This demand drives customers' inventory management, which in turn drives purchasing. For the customer, the cost of purchasing these relatively small products that come in small job lots can be substantial because of the number of purchases made of such relatively small items, and the amount of paperwork involved. Handling costs (making receipts, quality checks, unpacking, etc.) are equally onerous. A study found that ordering and handling costs for a typical industrial customer amounted to more than 100 FIM per order line—equal to the actual cost of many order lines. As a result, the customer has to choose between ordering fasteners in larger lots and holding unnecessary inventory, or paying the price of multiple small orders.

Würth Oy's original value proposition lay in offering the right fastener and assembly solutions for metal engineering companies through an extensive field sales force that met face-to-face with the customer (i.e., an offer to purchase). But over the past 10 years, just-in-time success stories from Japan and the United States prompted Finnish customers to seek streamlined purchasing solutions.

In response, Würth began to design stores next to the customers' assembly line, a move that reduced customers' purchasing and material handling costs and improved assembly line operations.

Today, Würth Oy operates these stores for over 1,000 customers in Finland. The stores are replenished on average

(continued)

RECONFIGURING THE SUPPLY-DEMAND CHAIN (CONTINUED)

twice a week by Würth's field sales force, totally eliminating the purchasing and handling costs for the customer. (An additional 10,000 customers have used the idea to operate their own on-site stores—they order replenishments and stock the shelves themselves.)

At the heart of the proposition is an offer to planning. By collaborating with the customer on the shop floor where maintenance is carried out and alterations to assembly line operations planned, Würth Oy's representatives know exactly what the customer will be needing and can keep the right stock of products on hand.

The benefit for the customer is obvious: A typical industrial customer saves a minimum of 70 FIM in purchasing and handling costs for each ordered item. Würth has also benefited: It is able to charge a 40 FIM premium on its products compared with the lowest cost (offer-to-purchase) competitor on the average order line. However, setting up and managing these in-plant stores is complex, and relatively expensive. Even with the price premium, it is not easy to make a profit simply by moving the VOP. However, moving the VOP also gave Würth the opportunity to move the OPP and so make its own supply chain much more efficient.

Earlier access to customer demand information has enabled it to consolidate shipping (by moving the OPP from local service centers to a national distribution center), but still make deliveries in a timely manner. More accurate information has also enabled Würth to reduce safety stocks and streamline sourcing. Indeed, customer demand information is gathered so early and accurately that Würth is even considering moving the OPP back still further in the demand chain to its own suppliers.

Cases like that of Würth indicate the enormous advantages available even to suppliers of commodity goods who think carefully about how to change the points on the demand-supply chain at which they offer value and take demand from their customers. The experience of Würth's competitors offers a pretty good idea of what can happen to those who fail to do so. To compete with Würth in Finland, they have been forced to cut their prices, which then forces them to cut costs and further undermines their service and value added offering to the customer.

symmetrically. Instead of thinking either "What can I do for the customer?" (as in marketing) or "How can I be more effective?" (as in operations) you can think "How can I reduce costs by offering higher value to the customer?"

How do you do this? There are five basic steps:

1. Identify the customer's demand chains. (Note that a customer can have a number of different demand chains.)

2. Define the potential linkage points for the supplier to the customer demand chains. (What are the potential VOPs?)

3. Identify your extended supply chains.

4. Define the potential linkage points for the customer to the supply chains. (What are the potential OPPs?)

5. Try out the possible configurations and evaluate the cost and benefit for yourself and the customer. (Are there win-win solutions?)

To return to our nuts-and-bolts example, Würth found that their industrial customers needed fasteners for three basic reasons. In their operations, the customer uses fasteners to assemble their own products. In aftersales, fasteners are needed for service and repair, and finally fasteners are needed to maintain plant and equipment used to make the products.

For each of these uses the demand chain is different. The demand chain for fasteners in the customer's assembly operations starts with production engineering and planning, followed by inventory management and purchasing. In the service demand chain, the need for fasteners is determined by service calls to customers, and in the plant maintenance chain by preventive service schedules and procedures for how to respond to machine breakdowns.

Step 2 is to find your potential value offering points. Focusing on the assembly operation of the customer, Würth realized that there are three points in the demand chain where a supplier can offer value: production planning, inventory management, and purchasing. The goal for an offer to planning would be to improve the productivity of the assembly operation. For an offer to inventory management, the focus would be to make sure that fasteners do not run out, and for an offer to purchasing, it would simply be to deliver as quickly and accurately as possible according to the customer's order.

Step 3 is to identify the extended supply chain. In supplying fasteners to an assembly line, the extended supply chain consists of production, warehousing, transport to the customer, making the fasteners accessible for the assembly operation, and finally using the fastener for assembling the customer's product.

Step 4 is to define the points where customer demand can link in to the supply chain. In the case of fasteners, the number of different products is large. This makes it very difficult to put the order penetration point at the transport stage (but if there were only a few different products, or the product could be customized on the fly, then we could also consider transportation for the OPP location). Thus, the points where customer demand can be allocated to products are production, warehousing, and the customer's own assembly operation.

The final step is configuring the demand-supply chain. In the fastener example, the key to reducing costs by offering higher value to the customer is in the assembly plant of the customer.

By designing an in-plant store that is easily accessible and close to the assembly line or cell, Würth helps the customer improve productivity in its assembly operations. The trick is to keep the in-plant store stocked with exactly the right range of fasteners for the mix of products being assembled. To do this, the service representative needs to collaborate with the customer as they make changes to the assembly operation (e.g., introduce new products and change the construction of current ones). An additional benefit for the customer of Würth's offer to planning is that it is not necessary to include the fasteners in the purchasing bill of materials. Würth takes full responsibility for providing the assembly operation with an accessible and well-managed supply of fasteners (see Figure 4.4).

The field service representative takes care of all inventory management, replenishment orders, and shelving on his route. Big customers with many in-plant stores are served by a representative who spends all his time in the customer's plant, while customers with only a few in-plant stores are visited every other day or even just once a week.

The regular visits and the focus on the customer's assembly operation are also the key to improving the supplier's efficiency. Instead of striving to increase short-term sales, the field sales force is in fact focusing on creating a more stable and predictable demand. A more even flow of replenishment orders makes it possible to reduce safety stocks. And, simply by regularly monitoring demand, the supplier gets more time to react, and can consolidate his own stocks. For example, an in-plant store is typically visited once or twice a week.

This means that Würth has at least 36 hours to respond, and can move the inventory back in the supply chain (no more need to keep retail or local distribution centers to serve the assembly customers). In fact, Würth has set up a single distribution center for the whole country, which is optimized for fast stock turnover and efficient picking and packing. Moving the OPP from 50 local service centers to a common distribution center cuts inventory buffers for

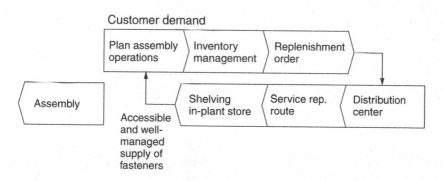

Figure 4.4   Delivery of a Fastener Supplier's Value Offering to an OEM's Assembly Operation

Würth to roughly one seventh of the original level. Competitors using an offer-to-purchase model face much tighter constraints, with customers expecting overnight delivery or off-the-shelf availability within a convenient distance.

By moving the VOP to planning, Würth has bought itself time to move the OPP to a national distribution center. This configuration increases the value to the customer and at the same time enables the supplier to improve supply chain efficiency.

The latest development is to cut out one visit from the time needed to replenish the in-plant store. The solution is the smart shelf that the company is developing with a few of its biggest customers. The smart shelf is an in-plant store with two bins for each item. On the second bin, a micro switch is mounted, which triggers a mobile phone modem to send a replenishment signal to the distribution center. The next time the representative visits the in-plant store, she can have the replenishment with her, cutting out one visiting cycle for the replenishment of the items. Then, how can Würth use the additional time to react? For items that are unique to a particular in-plant store, the obvious benefit is to order these items from the manufacturer or the Würth Group's other European distribution centers. With several thousand such items, Würth can again cut the risk of obsolescence in its own operation significantly.

A solution that integrates both demand and supply makes it difficult for competitors to win over your customers. For example, e-purchasing is not a serious threat for Würth in Finland. Transaction costs in the demand chain can be reduced through e-purchasing, but since Würth also manages the physical flow, (reduces handling and improves assembly efficiency), e-purchasing cannot provide comparable value to the customer. The most serious competition for Würth in Finland comes from local entrepreneurs who set up in-store plants for companies in a specific area. However, no national or international competitor has so far been willing to make the investment to challenge Würth in Finland. Such a challenge will become increasingly difficult, due to the switching costs for industrial customers.

Chapter

Excellence through Demand-Supply Chain Management

By coordinating your order penetration and value offering points, you can find new solutions to many difficult operational issues (e.g., how to replace inventory with information and how to launch new products more effectively).

What can we achieve with demand-supply chain management? The remainder of this chapter shows how it can be applied to tackle some widely spread, and difficult operational situations:

- ➤ How to replace inventory with information in distribution.
- ➤ How to simplify materials administration in assembly and manufacturing.
- ➤ How to launch new products or campaigns (without having too little product in the beginning and too much in the end).
- ➤ How to exceed the expectations of an old customer.
- ➤ How to find completely new value offerings.
- ➤ How to find the right combination of value offerings for a new business.

■ REPLACE INVENTORY WITH INFORMATION IN DISTRIBUTION

Take a look at almost any sales organization or purchasing organization, and you will find that the low-volume items cause most problems with high inventory levels and unanticipated shortages. Consider, for example, the demand-supply chain for packaged consumer goods.

The supply chain starts with materials suppliers that provide the ingredients and packaging materials for the grocery supplier's manufacturing and packaging. The next step is then distribution, which often includes a network of finished goods warehouses on the supplier side. The retailer (or the wholesaler that she uses) may likewise have a number of warehouses that finally deliver the goods to the retail stores, where the product is displayed on shelves for the consumer to purchase.

The retailer's demand chain consists of assortment planning or category management, inventory management, and purchasing.

The demand-supply chain configuration is the basic setup. The packaged consumer goods supplier makes his offering to purchasing, and the supplier allocates the product to the retail customer based on the customer's purchase order in a distribution center.

For small product quantities, the purchasing, goods receipt, and invoice verification on the retailer side, together with the order administration and picking on the supplier side can be 10 times more expensive than shipping full pallets. As a consequence of high ordering and delivery costs, low-volume items are ordered more infrequently than high-volume items, even though consumption often is just as even. The typical response for a supplier is to classify items in three categories: "A" for the 20 percent of items that sell 80 percent of the total, "B" for the next 30 percent, and "C" for all the remaining slow-moving items. The fast moving "A" items are targeted for high service levels, while occasional disruptions are accepted for the slow movers.

However, the customer requirement for delivery service for slow-moving items can be the same as for fast movers. To respond to such customer requirements for delivery service, the supplier may consider investing in higher safety stocks for the slow-moving products. But you don't have to accept safety stocks as the only solution to improve service.

The problem is that in the product range, lower rank products are ordered less often, even though they might be consumed at a constant rate. For fast-moving products, the supplier gets information on demand every day (daily orders), but for a slow-moving product only occasionally (an order every month or two). Put another way, for fast-moving products the daily consumption is passed on daily to the supplier, while for slow-moving items it is aggregated over time.

The key parameters when determining safety stock are average demand and the variation in demand. So, the supplier that gets occasional orders will need a higher safety stock than one that receives daily orders.

Now, suppose the supplier got the same quality information—daily consumption—for all products. This would mean that the supplier would have more time to react for all but the most high-volume products, which don't cause problems anyway because they are already ordered daily. Instead of having the slow-moving items physically in stock, the product could be on the way in manufacturing, or packaging.

But, how can a supplier get this "time profit" and replace inventory with information?

The answer is to stop relying on purchase orders: The manufacturer of packaged consumer goods needs to move VOP from purchasing to inventory management in the customer's demand chain. But there is also more to it. To deliver all products with the same efficiency by replacing inventory with information, the supplier needs to take three basic steps:

1. Move the VOP to inventory management; move up the customer's demand chain by replacing purchase orders. You can do this, for example, by replenishing the customer daily, based on the customer's inventory report. The result is that the information on customer demand is equally good for all products. For all but the most high-volume products, this gives the supplier more time to react, a time profit.

2. Use the time profit to reduce the customer's costs. For example, offer assured availability to the customer, or bill to consumption to simplify the customer's accounts payable process. (This reduces the customer's costs because she can verify her accounts payable against total goods issues, or sales.)

3. Use the time profit to improve your performance and maybe to increase product differentiation. For example, moving the OPP to pack to order gives more variety to lower cost for the supplier.

➤ Move the VOP to Inventory Management

To move even closer to customer demand in the grocery supply chain, a manufacturer of packaged consumer goods might try to use scanning data from the supermarkets (i.e., points of sale) to automatically replenish. But, there are practical obstacles. Scanning data is often unreliable: At checkouts not all items are scanned. For a consumer buying three varieties of potato chips—all priced the same—the checkout might just scan one and multiply by three. Over time, even small errors accumulate and lead to a stockout that is not identified until an inventory count is made.

Another problem is the timing and speed for collecting scanning data from a large number of points of sales. Aggregating offline tens of thousands of scanning events from thousands of shops takes time and can delay an accurate consumption report by weeks. Aggregating the data online again requires that all points of sales be continuously linked to the same monitoring application. Online aggregation of scanning data is a Web-based service that won't be widely adopted until the "pay-by-scan" setup is commonplace. Here the retailer does not pay the supplier until the product is sold to the consumer. But to be a win-win configuration, the supplier needs timely access to the scanning data and be able to replace inventory by information in the supply chain.

Another option for the manufacturer is to opt for a simpler solution and monitor how goods leave wholesaler or retailer distribution centers. Here, purchase orders are replaced with an inventory report that the supplier receives or accesses regularly. This vendor managed inventory (VMI) solution can be extremely simple and robust. The customer shares his "free stock" information once every day. Free stock means that the next day's deliveries to the retailers are already subtracted from the wholesaler's or distributor's inventory level. By replenishing the distribution center daily, the stock levels can be kept very low for the high-volume products. For the low-volume products, the supplier can reduce his own stocks because he sees the daily demand instead of purchase orders weekly, or even less often.

Figure 5.1 shows the result from a VMI implementation in the grocery supply chain. The graph shows how much more time to react the supplier gets when weekly orders are replaced with a daily inventory check. In this graph, amplification is a measure of how much the demand information was distorted. The demand amplification scale starts at one, which means that the demand that the supplier sees through purchase orders is identical to the demand the retailer actually experiences. The higher the amplification, the more purchase orders and actual demand are out of synch.

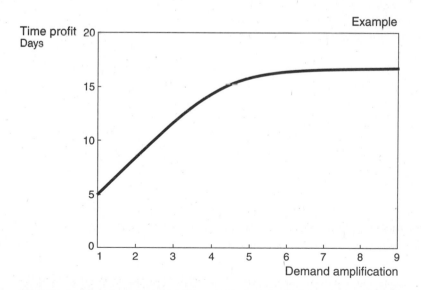

Figure 5.1 Time Profit from Moving VOP to Inventory Management

For items where purchase orders did not distort demand, the time profit when moving from weekly orders to daily inventory count is five days—the inventory count is like getting five orders a week instead of one. However, for the items with higher amplification, the replacement of weekly purchase orders with inventory reports gives much more time than could be achieved by daily orders. The inventory count gives the supplier up to three more weeks' time—15 working days—to react at the same level of delivery service. Before, for items purchased infrequently by the retailer, the information about variations in the end consumer demand was delayed and amplified by the retailer's purchasing organization. With the VMI solution, the supplier can monitor the demand at the retailer's.

Time profit can be understood as move away from a situation where you always need to be able to deliver in case the customer makes an order. And, you move to a situation where you do not need to do anything—not keep the product in stock, nor scheduled in your production plans—as long as the customer has enough. For products where the minimum delivery quantity is large in comparison to the daily consumption rate of the customer, the supplier can simply monitor the customer's inventory and start replenishing when there is just enough time to complete the next delivery before the first one runs out.

➤ Use the Time Profit to Reduce the Customer's Costs

Replacing purchase orders with a daily inventory report or point-of-sales data gives the supplier information of the same quality for all products, regardless of the sales volume. The next step for the supplier is to determine what to do with this time profit. As a supplier, you need to think carefully about this. Your customer will only change the way he buys from you if there are clear benefits for him.

For a retailer, the benefit of an offer to inventory management (i.e., a supplier responding to inventory reports rather than purchase orders) is that there will be fewer lost sales and outdated products. A 1996 study by the Coca-Cola Retailing Research Council found that in the grocery supply chain, the average item is out of stock one out of twelve times that a consumer visits a store. The stockouts translate into lost sales of 5 percent for the supplier, and 3 percent for the retailer (consumer makes an alternative purchase).

When we shift attention away from the average grocery retailer to other retail formats, we find that for mass merchants the problem is significantly bigger than for smaller formats. The incidence of stockouts for promotional items can be as high as one in five. The simple reason is that mass merchants have a wider product range than supermarkets or category killer shops. And, the incidence of stockouts increases faster than the product range because of the complexity of the control task.

The problem of lost sales is an issue, even for commodity goods such as groceries, but is a major problem in more innovative product categories. For products such as sporting goods, personal computers, apparel, and books eliminating stockouts would typically increase sales between 20 and 25 percent for the supplier, while for the retailer the figure is half of that. Even though a retailer can frequently guide the customer to buy another product, the risk is that the consumer loses patience and takes her shopping elsewhere. The point is that the time profit from better information is an opportunity for the retailer to become the preferred place to shop for consumers who have been disappointed elsewhere.

A supplier that wants to move away from purchase orders thus needs to show that his offer to manage inventory for the retail customer reduces stockouts and increases sales. That is, the time profit will be used for the benefit of the retail customer; the supplier takes responsibility for minimizing stockouts, and through this action helps the retailer to increase sales and the service to the end consumer.

Markdowns and obsolescence are other issues that can be attacked by moving the value offering point to inventory management. For example, a European confectionery manufacturer found that in several markets up to 10 percent of the volume purchased by the local sales and marketing organization became stale and could not be sold. There was a continuous struggle to push product out to retailers before the best-before date. And, because the taste of chocolate deteriorates over time, the company also had trouble maintaining its reputation as a supplier of quality chocolate.

However, moving the supplying factory's value offering point to inventory management in the sales and marketing organization's demand chain, quickly resolved the problem. Instead of purchasing orders, the sales and marketing organizations started to send a daily inventory report, and a weekly update of their sales forecasts (note: sales to their customers, not forecast of orders to the supplying factory). Based on this, the factory simply replenishes inventory up to the forecasted sales for the next two weeks. If sales are higher than expected, then the inventory report will immediately trigger new shipments. And, if sales are lower than the forecast, more products will not be shipped until they are actually needed.

The results were dramatic and immediate. In the pilot market, obsolescence costs decreased from 8 percent to 4 percent of sales in the first year, and again to 2 percent in the second year. At the same time, product availability for promotions and seasonal peaks improved as a result of the planning collaboration between sales and production. An additional benefit was that the efforts of the local supply managers could be redirected to improving sales forecasts and service to retail customers. And, maybe most importantly, the chocolate reaching the consumer is fresh, which helps increase consumer demand and improve the brand image.

Moving away from purchase orders can also reduce customer's costs by streamlining the demand chain and by shifting tasks to the supplier. However, it is not only by eliminating purchasing that the customer can realize cost savings. The pay-by-scan solution already mentioned simplifies the invoice verification, and payment process. The customer can easily verify and execute payments to the supplier based on his own sales.

The issue of becoming locked in with the supplier's solution is frequently an obstacle for moving away from purchase orders. But since most customers even in the future will need a purchasing process to deal with a great number of other suppliers, it is rarely a problem in reality. If a customer for some reason wants to go back to a more arm's-length relationship, it is much simpler to start with purchasing orders again than it was to set up the collaborative process in the first place. The customer retains her buying power, the only question is where in the demand chain it is executed. In an arm's-length relationship, it is executed on the transactional level; in a collaborative relationship it is executed when products are introduced, assortments are changed, and so on.

➤ Use the Time Profit to Improve Supplier Performance

Finally, the third step is to leverage the time profit for better supply chain performance and possibly more product differentiation. Replacing inventory with information by reducing safety buffers is only a first step. Because the supplier has more time to react, he can choose to move the OPP back in the supply chain. For example, there is no need to keep distribution centers as close to the customers as before, which means that the supplier can more easily centralize his own warehousing.

Additionally, with more time to react, there is no need to always have all products in stock—especially customer-specific items. It is enough that the replenishment reaches the customer before there is a stockout in the customer's inventory. For example, a packaged consumer goods supplier can pack-to-order special displays that a specific customer uses to promote sales or to simplify shelving in the store. Through this service, the supplier acquires the capability to make a completely new offer to the customer—an offer to planning where the supplier can propose to help the customer reduce handling costs and increase sales.

In the European market, with dozens of national and local languages, a supplier of nonperishable consumer goods faces a complex task if he wants to serve the whole market from specialized production plants. For exactly the same product and brand (e.g., washing detergent), the supplier needs different packages. The complication is that with traditional packaging, it is not possible to produce for all markets with the same frequency. For example, a product destined for the German market can be produced every week, while for the Finnish market only every other month. This means that even with a substantial time profit from moving away from purchase orders, the factory is too inflexible to respond. And, inventory cannot be replaced by information.

By adopting print-on-demand technology for packaging materials, however, it is even possible to use the time profit for efficiently offering retail customers' private labels. A simple first step is to separate containers from labels. Products destined for all markets can then be packaged before they are allocated to different markets, or retail customers. The second step is to then label them based on replenishment orders from different markets, or customers. The result of this VOP/OPP setup (offer-to-inventory management and label-to-order) is that the supplier does not need to carry any inventory of finished goods "just in case." At the same time, retail customers in small markets and customers with private labels can be offered the same availability as customers for the highest volume products in the major markets.

The complication with using collaborative offerings to improve supply chain performance, is that you cannot switch to a new VOP with all customers at the same time. This means that from some customers you receive purchase orders, while for others you receive inventory reports and plans. However, benefits are incremental. Reducing demand surges from just one customer will synchronize the supplier better with the market. The bigger the customer is, the bigger the impact from synchronization will be. The impact is that there will be less need for safety buffers when demand varies less, and that less capacity reserves are needed to meet demand peaks. If capacity is not cut, it means that the service

HOW THE VMI ADOPTION RATE AFFECTS MANUFACTURING

How does vendor managed inventory (VMI) help a manufacturer to synchronize production with demand? Three factors make this possible:

1. *More level demand* Customers that order themselves batch demand in purchase orders. For some products, the ordered quantity will last the customer a few days, while for another it may be enough for several weeks. For the supplier (vendor), seeing the demand from the customer's customer directly (e.g., through a daily inventory count) reduces demand variation. Instead of getting an order intermittently for the different products, the supplier gets daily demand for all products.

2. *More level load on production* A more level demand means a more level load on production. This is best seen by how much extra capacity and finished goods inventory a supplier needs to meet customer demand. Thanks to the reduced variability of demand, a supplier does not need to resort to buffering when capacity utilization increases. For VMI customers, the inventory buffer needed to maintain the same level of delivery service increases only slowly when capacity utilization increases from 75 to 90 percent. Only when utilization goes beyond 90 percent does the supplier need to start buffering to maintain the service level.

3. *More Capacity Available to Service Non-VMI Customers* When it is easier to meet demand for VMI customers, it automatically also becomes easier to meet demand for non-VMI customers. The reason for this is that fewer unexpected large orders from VMI customers leave more room to respond to the orders from other customers. This effect is already present at a very low level of VMI adoption but increases steadily with the adoption rate.

The result is that many grocery suppliers already with 40 percent of demand through VMI can produce 95 percent of the total volume in sync with market demand.

to all customers can be improved while buffers are reduced. This positive feedback effect is the reason Campbell Soup is able to produce 95 of its products in synchronization with demand, with an offer to inventory management of only 40 percent of the total sales. Other companies implementing vendor managed inventory solutions in the grocery supply chain have discovered the same. With an offer to inventory management of less than half of the total volume, the major benefits for the supplier are already realized.

■ SIMPLIFY THE CUSTOMER'S MATERIALS ADMINISTRATION WITH AN OFFER TO PLANNING

Making an offer to the customer's inventory management works well in the grocery supply chain. But, what about situations where managing the inventory is not the primary concern for the customer? A retailer that runs out of one product does not have to close the shop. But if your customer assembles products to sell, then she might have to stop or reschedule even if only one little part is missing.

To reschedule assembly is tricky. Different end products often use the same parts and materials. This means that if you change the schedule today because you have run out of one component, the change might cause a shortage of another tomorrow. You can try to get more from a supplier on short notice so that you can keep your operation going. The problem is that when the supplier reschedules, a new part will be delayed and require more quick fixes. And, all this activity is just for dealing with the problems caused by one missing part. A supplier with a value offering that enables the customer to responsively assemble the products the markets require can indeed add value.

Stocking plenty of components is one possibility for the supplier, but replacing inventory with information would be better. How do you replace inventory with information in assembly industries (e.g., automobiles, computers)? One option is making an offer to material requirements planning. Another is to adjust the offer to inventory management to account for interdependencies between different items.

➤ Replace Purchase Orders with the Bill of Material and End Product Demand

Internally, assembly and manufacturing companies use the bill of materials (BOM) to manage the information about the components needed for specific assemblies. However, most suppliers deliver individual components, each maybe with a different lead time and in different lot sizes. If you change the schedule, or even an individual order, the requirements for each and every component used in the assemblies also change. That means a lot of different purchases to check, and possibly to reschedule. In effect, a small change in demand or schedule for the end product causes an avalanche of checking and changes on the component and supplier level.

The solution is for the supplier to move the focus from the purchase order and item requirements to the bill of material and end product demand. Delivering a set of components according to the BOM of the end products immediately improves responsiveness. The parts needed for a specific end product are delivered in equal proportions to actual demand, and with the same lead time. Now, a change in demand for the end product can be handled with a single change in the supply of the component set instead of a large number of changes in different purchase orders.

However, the components are needed in the physical assembly of the product. This means that the supplier can add more value by delivering the components not only at one time, and in the right proportions, but as a kit. A kit includes the components needed for one assembled product. The key for moving the VOP to requirements planning is on the supply chain side kitting, and on the demand chain side the bill of material. Avnet, a U.S. electronic components distributor, is a company that has successfully developed an offer to requirements planning based on kitting according to the customer's bill of material.

➤ Adjusting the Offer to Inventory Management for Dependent Demand

Vendor managed inventory has proved to be an effective, yet simple tool, to better meet distributor and retailer demand. Is it possible to find a comparable solution for the demand chains of manufacturers and assembly operations?

The 3C (capacity, commonality, consumption) materials management system, developed by Enrique Lopez-Tello, Xavier Gurrola-Gal, and Miguel Fernandez-Ranada[1] at Lucent Technologies exhibits interesting features that can be adjusted to make an offer to inventory management for dependent demand.

The background to the 3C approach is incessant complaints from sales on the performance at the Lucent plant in Tres Cantos, Spain, where Miguel Fernandez-Ranada was plant manager. Instead of ignoring the problem or simply investing in better scheduling software Fernandez-Ranada started to look for possible solutions together with Lopez-Tello, a supply chain specialist, and Gurrola-Gal, a Bell Labs Fellow.

The existing best-practice alternatives were found lacking. Demand management by freezing the demand horizon was difficult due to frequent late changes from sales and customers. Forecasting accuracy was even more difficult to improve to a level where components could be accurately secured from suppliers with long lead times in the United States and Japan. And, more frequent planning cycles were no solution, either. Frequent replanning would simply generate too many changes.

Instead, a new approach was developed. The principle is to plan the business (sales) based on capacity, leverage commonality to reduce inventory, and produce according to consumption (actual demand).

The first step is to define a maximum sales rate of each end product that the factory will support. Second, the factory capacity to produce the end product (units of output per day) is determined. And finally, the component level maximum daily usage rate is defined.

The maximum daily usage rate on the component level is set in three steps. First, the maximum sales rates for the end products that use the component are checked. If there is plenty of capacity to assemble all end products that use the component, then the usage rate for the component is calculated from the sales rates of the end products. If there is not enough capacity, then the usage rate for the component is calculated according to the greediest mix of end products. In other words, assume that the end product that consumes most of the component per unit of time is produced to the maximum sales rate. Then, the one that uses the next biggest quantity of the component is also produced to the maximum sales rate, and so on, until the factory capacity is all used up. This way, when capacity is the constraint, increasing the commonality of components in the end products increases demand for the specific component. But it reduces the total requirements for components (because you don't need more components than you have the capacity to use).

This sounds complicated, but it is really simple. The point is that the maximum daily rates on both the component level and end product level are calculated quarterly, or even only annually. The only thing that is needed daily is to check the on-hand inventory, what is on the way from the suppliers, and make sure that the sum is bigger than the maximum usage rate for the number of days it takes the supplier to replenish. The supplier replenishes to consumption. Now, the supplier can with a high level of confidence promise that there will be enough components for whatever rescheduling the assembly plant does within the agreed limits. And finally, leveraging the component commonality and capacity constraints, inventory can be reduced up to 45 percent compared with conventional material requirements planning (MRP).

In the Lucent case, the assembly company kept control, but component suppliers can easily adapt the solution for moving the VOP. The goal is making an offer to inventory management—less inventory, lost sales, and obsolescence—for assembly demand. The daily operations are possible to synchronize with a very simple setup by redefining the terms of availability, based on a quarterly or annual collaboration process. The key for success is that the assembly customer must be willing to share, for each of the supplier's components, the end product sales rates and maximum capacity. And, on a daily basis, the customer sends an inventory report that is used to determine what needs to be replenished.

Why would a supplier go through the trouble to set up such collaboration? The advantages are better information, and a more stable demand for all components. There is no daily replanning by the customer, and no avalanches of changes for the supplier to react to.

From the customer viewpoint, the advantage is reduced work, lower inventory levels, and substantially better service. The role of forecast can be diminished for production and material requirements, and there is no need to allocate materials to products before they are actually needed in assembly.

The setup is fast and simple. The difficulty in making the offer is, again, convincing the customer in the first place that abandoning purchase orders and replacing them with a collaborative process really brings benefits.

■ COLLABORATING TO LAUNCH NEW PRODUCTS EFFICIENTLY

In launching a new product, there is always a significant risk for ending up with excess inventory; the risk is especially large for products with short life cycles. Surprisingly, with an offer to purchase, excess inventory is often the result whether the launch is successful or not.

If successful, there is initially a backlog in deliveries to customers anxious to purchase the product. This, in turn, leads to overheated sales forecasts. Finally, when supply catches up with demand, the backlog disappears and the inventory levels surge. In a situation where product life cycles are short, this excess inventory quickly becomes obsolescent.

If unsuccessful, large initial channel orders make the supplier reluctant to reduce the sales forecast. When the demand situation becomes clear, however, it is already too late to turn off supply.

➤ Reaching Different Value Offering Points

The opportunity here is that over the product life cycle—or the duration of a big sales promotion—the supplier can aim at different points in the customer demand chains (i.e., change the VOP). At the same time, the supplier also needs to adjust his own response (i.e., change the OPP).

An example is the launch of personal digital assistants (PDAs). The technology embedded within personal digital assistants is getting more and more versatile, both regarding hardware and software. Besides working as a stand-alone toolbox for business and leisure time, the latest makes and models provide access and integration also to the user's communities—e-mail, calendar, Internet, even wireless communication. All these features, combined with how they are delivered, create the opportunity for advanced value offerings for the customer's benefit.

The provision of such offerings is extremely challenging for the manufacturer. The technology is developing extremely fast, and the PDA can be characterized as a product with shorter and shorter life cycles. The capability to make and distribute turns is a major constraint for popular new models.

In a situation like this, an offer to inventory management alone (e.g., VMI), does not work. For example, a retailer or distributor that can make an agreement assuring availability—not volume—will be able to secure a higher proportion of available products. The result is that the supplier through prioritizing a customer will help him build market share on the expense of other customers. Also, such an arrangement will secede the power to the trade customer to decide what end users will get the sought-after product.

However, the changes are not only in technology, but also in the development of PDA applications to support the user's lifestyle and business. In the corporate segment, the pressures to customize the product are mounting. In addition to product delivery, the user has to be provided with access to the corporate-specific software and data repositories, such as customer and product data, even bid and order processing.

Moving the VOP to the consumer or business user creates an opportunity to better manage product introductions. The conventional supply chain is primarily via a retailer to the corporate customer, but it can also be direct from the supplier. There is also a possibility that a telecom operator or its partner, a telecom specialist distributor will take the lead in customer access. This is particularly likely for cases in which corporate customers highly value the communication capability of the PDA.

The choice is not irrelevant from the viewpoint of the PDA manufacturer. Direct access to corporate customers would maximize customer intimacy and minimize the costs associated with the intermediates. Direct end customer relationships could even boost the corporate segment as a whole due to the close relation to customer feedback, as Dell Computer has learned in the PC business. On the other hand, there is a risk for channel conflict with electronics distribution specialists that aim to control distribution and access to consumers. Operators in turn, intend to maximize their subscription and airtime revenues. The particular make of a PDA is of less interest in their viewpoint.

A closer look at end users (e.g., the corporate customer's demand chain) reveals that there are opportunities for the supplier that need not challenge the distributor's or operator's business interests. Corporate customers of PDAs issue the devices with communication capabilities primarily to employees who travel or are otherwise frequently out of the office. Managers, salespersons, or consultants can be more productive because they have access to e-mail, calendar, and communication wherever they are. The hiring of new staff, introduction of mobile office solutions and wireless applications, and replacement of outmoded or broken devices drive the demand.

An obvious opportunity for the PDA supplier is to make an offer to replace outmoded PDAs directly to the corporate customers. This offer to planning does not compete head-on with the operator selling the connection subscriptions. Also, if the upgrades are highly customized, the competence requirements and transaction costs for the electronics distributor to provide the service will quickly increase and move beyond the distributor's capabilities.

But what is in it for the PDA manufacturer? The benefit of making this offer is that demand for a new model in the critical first weeks of a product introduction becomes transparent; the effect of new PDA solutions can be discussed directly with the business end user. To deliver to plan, the manufacturer and customer can agree on a set of rules for how and when existing devices are outmoded, and how to replace them with new models. This gives valuable information on how new products are taken into use in an important market segment. The jointly agreed plan can also be used to directly trigger supply of products customized to corporate specifications.

The critical issue for the PDA supplier is getting customers to replace old devices with new and better ones. The VOP for managing PDA in use and replacement in a large corporation is very interesting when introducing new models because the supplier can act independently.

What opportunities are there then for collaboration between the manufacturer and the operator and distributor? The offering to equip new staff is critical for the success of the PDA supplier, but it cannot be developed without the provider of new applications and communication subscriptions. Therefore, partnering with operators and retailers and helping them move the VOP to equipping new staff is a better solution.

Based on the job description and planned starting date, the new employee can be equipped with the right device from the first day at work. The more complementing suppliers there are, the bigger the benefit becomes. From the customer perspective, a streamlined process would include not only the PDA but also a connection to desktop/laptop computing, e-mail account, and subscriptions to fixed/wireless communication. Here, to offer value for equipping new employees, the telecom operator is critical because the new employee needs new subscriptions in addition to the devices. The role of the electronics distributor does not change: The front/back end of the user's desktop/laptop computer has to be set up for PDA applications. Some user services also need to be set up on the corporate servers.

To sum up, what VOP does a manufacturer need to support more efficient product introductions? The key is to collaborate with the corporate customer on managing a standard for PDA including networking and communication. When a new product is launched, the corporate customer needs to decide whether and how it is to be used, and what the effect will be on the park of devices already in use. This decision is the basis for managing PDA devices and their applications in the company including the ordering and replacement processes. The supplier then can quickly and effectively introduce the new product in end user organizations that have a clear need for it and that may even have participated in the development of corporate-specific features.

The principle is to start directly with sophisticated consumers or corporate customers that replace outdated products with the new product, and then move on to channel partners. After a new product has been introduced to lead users, it is introduced also in the standard assortment of channel partners. But the focus is still on servicing the end users' replacement and new hiring demand. This way the manufacturer and channel partners can jointly make a credible offering that goes beyond purchasing.

➤ Support Product Introductions with Collaborative Planning

How can you collaborate efficiently with a large number of channel partners? The basis for collaborating with operators and retailers is to help each customer manage its "standard assortment" or "installed base." The assortment is used as a tool to periodically review the impact of new product introductions, sales campaigns, and pricing changes on the whole product range.

Conventional forecasting techniques—based on time series analysis—work well when the business situation is stable, but as soon as there is a need to react to a combination of changes, they do not measure up. For example, more frequent replanning, or the use of more detailed channel and customer sales figures just increases the workload. The effect of each change has to be evaluated product by product and cannot be automated without risking accuracy. As a result, the amount of work involved in planning increases rapidly in precisely those situations when the involvement of channel partners is most valuable. This in turn makes it difficult to find customers willing to invest the time and effort.

A solution is to change your whole approach to planning—to use the standard assortment as the basis—instead of the sales history of individual products. Focusing on changes in rank can do this. Put aside for a while the problem of forecasting how much of each product is needed, and consider how the product introduction, the customer projects or sales campaigns, and the pricing changes will affect the standard assortment of that particular customer. The task is now to put the products in rank order, based on what you know. And to do this is much simpler for the key account and his counterpart on the customer side. Depending on how many products a supplier carries, the rankings can be done reliably in a matter of hours, while at the same time discussing customer plans and requirements.

Once the rank order of the standard assortment is set, the focus can return to what that means in terms of sales. For a rough estimate, the 80/20 rule can be used to translate rank to sales: You scale total sales to the products using a simple function that assigns a percentage of the sales to each rank. For more accurate results, you can use historical analysis to define an exact scaling function and adjust that to the anticipated changes. For example, heavy promotion of high-volume products will increase the share for the top ranks.

The objective with planning collaboration is not to get exact forecasts to the last decimal, but to get a reliable forecast based on the best available information as early as possible. And, by focusing on simplicity, you can introduce it with as many customers as possible. If the planning collaboration is carried out when customers make their own plans for the future, the supplier can receive high-quality information months in advance. In the mobile phones demand-supply chain, an operator that quarterly plans how he wants to develop and manage his mobile communications business gives the supplier the time needed to prepare a reliable supply. By getting more time to adjust resource allocation in the supply chain, the supplier can improve ramp-up and ramp-down through collaboration.

➤ Linking Plans to Execution

The next step then is efficient sales, achieved by minimizing obsolescence and lost sales. This means using the information from collaborating on standard assortments, and product introductions to maximize sell-through and minimize inventory in the supply chain. By making an offer to inventory management—not purchasing—the supplier can avoid unnecessary buffers. This is especially important for low-volume products.

Focusing on sell-through, rather than on order fulfillment, will also reduce the time needed to balance supply to demand. With an offer to purchasing and short life-cycle products, the balance is frequently never found. This is also why the market success of a new product does not affect obsolescence and markdowns at the end of the cycle, and that both successful and unsuccessful launches result in obsolete inventory.

Figure 5.2 outlines the demand chain design for successfully linking business collaboration with channel partners to efficient replenishment for a supplier company. Product introductions, assortment changes, and promotions of the channel partners are used as the basis for collaboration. In the collaboration process, a shared forecast is created using the ranking and scaling approach, which in turn calibrates the supply chain. The actual product supply is triggered by sales, using, for example, a simple VMI solution to generate replenishment orders.

On a smaller scale, campaigns and promotions can be managed according to the same principles as new product introductions. Retailers' campaigns that wreak havoc when you

Business Plan	Sales Forecast	Control Parameter Settings	Order Generation
Category Management	Forecasting Collaboration	Supply Chain Planning Control	Vendor-Managed Inventory
Assortment Production introduction Promotion	Category ranking Category scaling Shared sales forecasts	Buffer locations Service levels Order lead times, buffer stocks, reorder points	Replenish based on inventory report (instead of order)

Figure 5.2 Demand Chain Activities Link Business Planning and Execution

are working with an offer to purchase can be identified in the collaborative demand chain. Based on the ranking, it is possible to account for the impact of the campaign on the assortment as a whole, and resources can be shifted smoothly from products that decrease in volume to those that need more resources.

➤ Minimizing the Supplier's Risk

The last step is for the supplier to minimize his own costs and risk, as well as to increase variety. The tool for this is moving the OPP from "ship-to-order" to "assemble-to-order" or "pack-to-order."

In many situations, a ship-to-order setup is necessary to introduce a product to all channel partners at the same time. The finished goods buffer is also needed by the supplier to keep a high service level. Fast delivery and reliability reduce the incentive for channel partners to build their own safety stocks. Building up safety stocks in the channel is a waste from the supplier perspective because end customers are waiting for the product.

With a VOP to inventory management, however, it is possible to move the OPP to assembly, as soon as capacity is sufficient to meet demand. This way you can start increasing product variety for the customers without facing excessive obsolescence risks. If you have not reached this VOP when starting to increase product variety for a new product introduction, you will have difficulty capturing all potential sales and risk increasing the end-of-cycle costs. Sport Obermayer, a supplier of winter sportswear, found that moving back the OPP for fashion items in its product line (a third of the items) reduced stock-out and markdown costs to only 5 percent of sales (from 11%).

When launching seasonal product lines, collaboration with end customers and channel partners is extremely valuable for identifying which products are most unpredictable. This information can then be used as the basis for choosing which items are assembled to order and which are shipped to order. In a similar way, Dell uses corporate customers' standards revision cycles to determine in advance the components for which it needs to secure scarce supply.

■ EXCEED THE EXPECTATIONS OF A KEY CUSTOMER

How do you exceed the expectations of an old customer? Simply because it is a well-established relationship does not mean that there are few opportunities. On the contrary, it is often easier to make innovative breakthroughs with an established customer.

The key is to understand the customer demand chain and to identify the potential new value offering points. With big industrial customers, Würth in Finland operates with an offer to planning—managing and replenishing fastener stores on the assembly line or in the production cell of the customer.

Kone Elevators, a manufacturer of elevators, was one of the first customers to adopt Würth's offer to planning. The company also played a key role in helping to perfect Würth's in-plant store and business concept. However, Kone does not only use fasteners in the assembly of new elevators, but also for aftersales. Here, service technicians use fasteners when performing preventive maintenance and repairs on Kone elevators around the country. When fastener supply for aftersales became an issue, the service technicians operated from local service depots. Spare parts were supplied to the depots from Kone's own distribution center, and the fasteners by Würth.

In addition to large industrial customers, Würth also has 15,000 small business customers in Finland. These simply want to purchase fasteners from Würth. For this purpose, Würth has established a network of retail outlets around the country. These outlets opened up quite an unexpected new value offering to Kone's aftersales demand chain.

Kone has been able to eliminate its own depots and spare-parts inventories around the country by partnering with Würth. Würth offers its retail outlet as the delivery address for spare parts needed by Kone's service technicians around the country. The parts are shipped from Kone's spare-parts center to Würth's retail outlets according to the service and maintenance assignments of the field service technicians. Kone's service technicians then come to one of Würth's retail outlets to pick up the parts needed to complete their assignments and at the same time stock up on fasteners (see Figure 5.3).

The cost savings for the customer are substantial from closing down service depots around the country. For Würth, there is no additional cost, only more sales. The parts are picked up the same day or the day after they arrive. Würth does no administration or information handling; it just provides a delivery address. However, with this simple action, the company was able to make a valuable offer to Kone's aftersales demand chain.

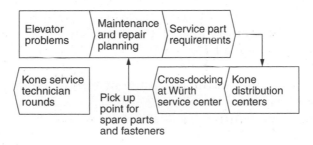

Figure 5.3   Aftersales Demand-Supply Chain

The evolution of the value offerings in Finland has followed its own path, but the global presence of Würth Group makes it possible for customers to transfer successful practices to other parts of the world. Kone Elevators has repeatedly transferred best practices from its collaboration with Würth in Finland to plants in other parts of Europe and in the United States.

Another company that leverages its direct relationship with business customers to develop new value offerings is Dell Computer. Normally, Dell's value offering is to the planning of a corporate standard for computer hardware and desktop applications. However, large corporate customers have many different demand chains for computers including equipment for new employees. Today, Dell has also implemented an offer to personnel planning with some established corporate customers. The objective is to supply, without purchase orders, the right computer for new employees based on advance information on starting dates and job requirements.

For whom is this new value offering? Consider a fast growth high-tech company that hires hundreds of people every year. Such a customer does not want to shop around for PCs for each new employee. And, the company won't impress a new hire who has to wait days to be connected to the company network. Such a corporate customer simply wants the new employee to have the PC she needs on her desk when she starts.

For this demand chain, Dell has developed a specific value offering. A local IT support provider visits the customer organization regularly. The service provider gets the list of starting dates for new employees from the human resources department as well as specifications for the PCs they need for their work. The service provider then does the purchasing and follow-up through the Premier Pages of the customer company and makes sure the right PC is in the right place on the right day.

Dell has also developed similar setups for replacement projects. These corporate customers want to minimize their own involvement in executing replacement and update projects. In Finland, the Dell offer is a service provider working with the IT organization in planning the replacement project and then executing it to plan.

■ FIND COMPLETELY NEW VALUE OFFERINGS

The demand-supply chain can also be used to find completely new value offerings. A key point here is that in addition to the customer demand chain, there may be a decision maker's demand chain.

Take McGraw-Hill's book printing business in university campus stores. In the usual demand chain for supplying books to students, the bookstore decides what assortment of books to sell after consulting professors (assortment planning), decides the quantity of supplies needed (inventory management), and then orders supplies from the publisher. The publisher's VOP is a straightforward offer to purchase, and the OPP is the publisher's warehouse/distribution center (see Figure 5.4).

The system isn't that great for the retailer's customers, the students, because books are expensive, and often only parts of an entire book are required reading. If the bookstore has underestimated demand, students may have to wait a long time for their books as the publisher will have to make extra shipments. What can the publisher do (who wants to help himself by helping his customer, the retailer, help her

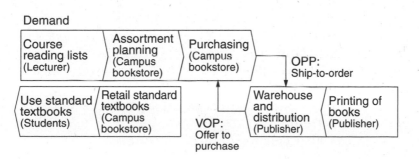

Figure 5.4 Traditional Demand-Supply Chain for Textbooks

customer, the student)? He starts by examining the whole supply-demand chain.

In this case, the retailer's assortment planning is driven by student demand, but that in turn is generated by the lecturer, who decides which textbooks he or she wants to use, and what other complementary reading materials are needed. So McGraw-Hill moved its value offering point back in the demand chain all the way to the point where the lecturer assembles a reading list, offering to provide a collection of reading material that matches the lecturer's requirements.

How does McGraw-Hill deliver this? By moving the OPP out of the warehouse to an assemble-on-demand model. McGraw-Hill's Primis electronic publishing system allows the lecturer to choose standard texts from a database and combine these with complementary material the lecturer himself supplies (see Figure 5.5). The tailored textbook, together with the lecturer's complementary material, is then printed in the bookstore on campus, where the students make the purchase.

The textbook that the student buys can be exactly adapted to the course that the lecturer gives—this is the primary value offering of the publisher to the lecturer; also, the textbook will be available with a much shorter lead time than in a conventional book supply chain.

For the student, the main benefit is price. In most cases the tailored textbook is cheaper than a standard mass-produced book because it includes only text that is required. Through

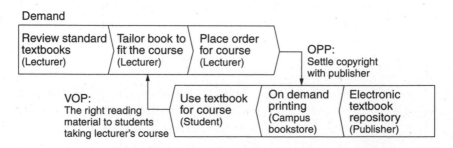

Figure 5.5   Primis Demand-Supply Chain for Textbooks

using on-campus printing technology, the unit cost is independent of batch size, thus removing obsolescence costs for the publisher (unsold books returned—up to 30 percent of sales) and opportunity cost for the retailer (wasted display space). Everyone wins.

McGraw-Hill is the largest U.S. custom publisher and has reached lecturers in over 1,400 university and college campuses with its new value offering. The success of this demand-supply chain configuration is best illustrated by the fact that several competitors are now following suit.

■ FIND THE RIGHT COMBINATION OF VALUE OFFERINGS FOR A NEW BUSINESS

So far, we have examined reshaping existing businesses using the demand-supply chain. But what if it is a completely new type of business—can you use the same tools to outline the opportunities? One such area where new value offerings are beginning to emerge through innovations in the supply-demand chain is electronic ordering of groceries (the e-grocery business). While this business is still in its infancy, it is becoming clear that new services are needed to make it a success. We can use the demand-supply chain to outline what these may be, and how they could be implemented.

In e-grocery today, the value to the consumer is the convenience of home shopping. But as the consumer also wants home delivery, retailers usually charge extra for the service. They might go some way to compensate for higher prices by using consumer information to tailor offers and so provide some kind of added value. But the offer still remains a basic offer to purchase, so any added consumer value is likely to be relatively small.

Because the VOP hasn't changed, the retailer does not get notification of demand until the consumer places the order, making it hard to extract extra efficiencies in the supply chain. The retailer still largely has to collect the items a consumer orders from the local supermarket shelf (the OPP hasn't changed). Moving the OPP by allocating, then delivering the order from a more distant warehouse might save on retail site costs and allow the retailer to offer wholesale prices, but delivery would take longer.

For a grocery consumer, the demand chain consists of all or some of the following steps: planning, inventory management, and purchasing.

The demand chain is different depending on the consumer and the product purchased. In the simplest case, the demand chain only consists of the purchasing step. A typical example of such a demand chain is a person shopping for groceries who suddenly decides to buy a candy bar just because she happens to see it displayed on the shelf.

A demand chain that includes inventory management in addition to purchasing is also common. In this case, the consumer first checks, for example, how much milk or juice is left in the refrigerator and based on this decides whether to buy some more.

Finally, the demand chain can also include all three activities: planning, inventory management, and purchasing. A consumer may first plan what the family will eat during the weekend, next check what ingredients are already in store, and then purchase the missing products. In some cases (e.g., the consumer is about to buy a new coffee machine), the inventory management step is not relevant and the demand chain activities only include planning and purchasing.

Planned demand (demand chains where the purchasing step is preceded either by planning or by inventory management) are estimated to account for about 40 to 55 percent of grocery purchases. There are, however, product categories where the amount of planned purchases is as high as 80 percent.

Suppose you ask a number of consumers to specify which products they usually purchase on impulse, which they replenish, and which they plan for some occasion? With the diversity of personalities, lifestyles, and the wide grocery product offerings, it will quickly become evident that one consumer can and should be approached with many different value offerings. And, it should be the consumer's choice that determines which products are supplied with which offering.

Moving the value offering point (the point in the demand chain at which the consumer allocates her demand to a specific supplier) provides a systematic approach to examining how an e-grocer can participate in the demand chain in novel ways. Next, we present three new potential value offerings that Johanna Småros[2] at Helsinki University of Technology has identified at different value offering points: Don't run out, plan and forget, and capture and enjoy.

➤ Don't Run Out—An Offer to Inventory Management

First consider what the online grocer Streamline has come up with. Streamline supplies and installs a special fridge in the consumer's garage where it can leave the consumer's order. This innovation improves on the offer to purchase in that the consumer doesn't have to be at home to take the delivery. However, a new service from Streamline called "Don't Run Out" goes further still. This service entails Streamline supplying what is basically a standing order for a selection of standard grocery products (e.g., milk, juice, pet food, diapers).

The consumer benefits from getting rid of reordering the same product week after week, but the e-grocer also benefits. The new service increases consumer loyalty toward both the e-grocer and the brands used. The demand perceived by the e-grocer also becomes stable and more predictable. This in turn provides new opportunities to arrange supplier shipments and order picking in a more efficient manner.

With Don't Run Out, Streamline is making an offer to inventory management. The problem is that it is impractical to include any other than the most basic weekly grocery shopping. Washing detergents and household cleaners are products that you don't want to have run out either. But depending on how busy you are, consumption may vary considerably.

What is needed is a way for the consumer to let the e-grocer monitor what is currently in stock by checking the kitchen. When looking at available technology to do this, there are no insurmountable hurdles. By actively collecting inventory data in the household, however, the amount of products covered by an offer to inventory management can be significantly increased.

The main issues are what data to use for controlling the replenishments and how to gather this information. The option used by Streamline is sending replenishments according to the consumer's buying profile (i.e., how the consumer has bought the products earlier on). Since this method relies on forecasting and extrapolation, it works for products with a steady consumption or perishable products that are thrown away when too old.

There are already existing solutions for tracking consumption in the household; Electrolux has developed a refrigerator equipped with a bar code scanner and Internet connection. Such flow control based solutions are attractive because they are easy to implement and use existing bar codes.

When looking beyond the surface, there are serious problems related to this approach. It requires active consumer participation in the product identification process: The consumer has to notify the data capture system each time an item is removed or added. This also makes the system inconvenient from the consumer's point of view. In addition, since the system relies on the consumer's actions to keep it up-to-date, it is prone to errors, and the errors accumulate.

Inventory count provides a more robust solution to the inventory data capture problem. Since the system relies on regularly checking what items are in stock instead of trying to keep track of a material flow, it is less error-prone. If errors occur, they are automatically corrected the next time an inventory count is performed. Also, the inventory counts can be automated, which makes the system more convenient for the user.

Different technologies can be used to implement an inventory count based data capture system. Radio frequency data collection (RFDC) is one of the most promising alternatives. Since RFDC technology is based on antennas and radio signals, no contact between the reader device and the items to be read is needed, making it possible to perform automated inventory checks without user interaction. For the system to work, however, all items covered by the vendor managed inventory service have to be marked with RF tags and the consumer's household equipped with a RF reader device.

The main problem in implementing such a system is the cost of the RF tags, approximately one dollar apiece, which is expensive compared with the virtually free bar codes. New consumable and potentially much less expensive tags have, however, recently been introduced, which could signify a breakthrough on the cost side. Another solution is recycling the tags. A tag that can be written and read several times costs between two and three dollars. The tag can be reused several thousands of times. Recycling the tag lowers costs significantly. Instead of two dollars, the cost to use the tag may only be a fraction of a cent.

➤ Plan and Forget—An Offer to Planning

Moving the value offering point even further in the consumer's demand chain, we arrive at a situation where the e-grocer actively supports the consumer's planning activities. The e-grocer can relieve the consumer from having to separately order each product needed for an occasion by reacting to the consumer's plans rather than to her orders. If the e-grocer also can take into account the inventory situation, the consumer is allowed to plan and forget, without risking ending up without important products and ingredients.

The idea behind plan and forget is similar to that of material requirements planning (MRP) used in the manufacturing industry. MRP systems allow companies to plan and schedule at the end product level, instead of at the component level. The MRP system automatically breaks down the plans to the component level, checks which components will be needed and when, performs inventory checks, and initiates purchase orders or call-offs from the supplier. Transposing this to the household environment means, for example, that consumers can specify an occasion on the meal level, rather than the ingredient level and simply plan a meal without having to check whether the required ingredients are in stock or having to order each ingredient separately. In the old days, this is what butlers did for their employers.

From the e-grocer's point of view, the benefits of plan and forget are similar to those of moving the VOP to the consumer's inventory management: better perception of the consumer's demand and more time to react to it. In addition, by providing the consumer with recipe databases, the e-grocer has the opportunity to affect the consumer's plans. Furthermore, the e-grocers obtain valuable information on how the consumers actually use different products.

The plan-and-forget concept can be implemented using existing technology. What is needed is a way for the e-grocer and consumer to plan collaboratively. This can be done using electronic Web-based calendars that can be accessed on the Internet. These calendars already exist and their importance will grow rapidly when more people start using wireless services. Recipe databases and Web-enabled grocery-ordering systems also are available. What is still required is linking these systems together in a secure, reliable, and convenient way.

An important point when considering the implementation of a plan-and-forget service, however, is that the system has to be able to somehow keep track of the current inventory situation as well as incoming goods. This means that the implementation of a full-blown plan-and-forget either has to be preceded by the implementation of a vendor managed inventory service or that the plan-and-forget system has to be extended to include also an inventory management component.

➤ Capture and Enjoy—Improve the Offer to Purchasing

Simply because products are on shelves in the bricks-and-mortar supermarket does not mean that virtual shelves are the best way for an e-grocer to display the product offering. There are several more ways for the e-grocer to do this. One alternative is especially interesting. This approach is based on using television in a new way that allows the consumers to "capture" things they see on TV and conveniently learn more about these selected items or instantly order them.

A capture-and-enjoy service does something traditional TV commercials cannot do: It makes shopping more efficient, and at the same time provides truly impulsive shopping and fun for the consumer. The fun aspect potentially comes from being able to peek into the cupboards, refrigerators, or wardrobes of the characters on the consumer's favorite TV shows. The efficiency comes from the consumer being able to instantly obtain more information on new products and to order immediately after making the decision.

The capture-and-enjoy concept can be implemented in several ways. Some attempts have, in fact, already been made to produce such a service. Microsoft has launched its Interactive TV concept: An icon appears on the TV screen when additional information is available and the consumer can then use the remote control to access it—the program and the information appear simultaneously on the screen.

Some important aspects of the capture-and-enjoy concept still need to be developed. First, the ordering mechanism has to be improved. Today, ordering products through Interactive TV is no easier than ordering through a Web page. Second, the consumer can only get additional information on products they see on commercials or on Web pages linked to the programs. The system is thus a lot less fun than if a consumer could actually peek into the closets of her favorite TV characters during a show. This aspect becomes especially important when looking at the potential offered by extending the product range from groceries to consumables such as shoes, clothes, and lingerie.

➤ A Mix of Value Offerings

In developing the e-grocery business model, the demand chain of consumers varies significantly depending on the products they purchase. However, which products have which demand chain is individual and changes with the situation. This means that a flexible mix of value offerings is crucial. This allows consumers to choose how they buy and when.

Also, the value offerings can be combined for an even bigger impact. For example, capture and enjoy can be linked to both Don't Run Out and plan and forget. Capture and enjoy then becomes a convenient way to select new products to include in the vendor managed inventory service or to entice the consumer to start planning an occasion. And, as mentioned, it is difficult to reach the full potential of plan and forget without a way of checking what the consumer already has available.

To turn e-grocery shopping into a serious challenger to the conventional model, e-grocers have to see beyond what has traditionally been done in grocery retailing. Instead of simply taking traditional retail formats and placing them on the Internet, e-grocers have to ask themselves: "What do our customers need and how can we fulfill these needs?" By systematically examining their customers' demand chains and developing value offerings that correspond to these chains, e-grocers can come up with new, meaningful services that increase the value of e-grocery shopping perceived by the consumer.

➤ Win-Win—Improve Value and Efficiency

With the Don't Run Out value offering, the consumer no longer has to make a weekly order of every item. And, with plan and forget, the consumer can focus on the occasion or task she wants to undertake, rather than the detailed planning. But at the same time, moving the VOP gives the e-grocer early access to demand information. Just as in the business-to-business situation, this brings opportunity to improve efficiency. It allows e-grocers to move the OPP from a supermarket or local shop, to a dedicated distribution center that can operate with much higher efficiency in order picking, distribution, and sourcing.

Once an order is fixed, Streamline can choose delivery times convenient to itself, because the reception box eliminates the need for the customer's presence. This is important, because the distribution efficiency can immediately be improved by 30 percent when the e-grocer can freely optimize the delivery route. And, more time to react also makes it easier for the e-grocer to purchase more efficiently from manufacturers and keep its own inventories low.

There are also opportunities for grocery manufacturers. The consumer receives an electronic record of her purchases from the e-grocer. This can easily be shared directly with supplier, if the consumer so chooses (much easier than a supermarket receipt). So what does this mean? It means that the grocery supplier can set up a loyalty scheme directly with the consumer. The basic idea is offering the consumer points for each purchase, exactly as airlines and hotels do. Extending the collaboration to the e-grocer, the consumer can then use the points for purchasing the supplier's product. But instead of rewarding opportunistic consumers, as coupons do, this type of promotion rewards the good customer. And, from an e-grocer perspective, the direct promotion by suppliers gives it a cost advantage over traditional supermarkets. The suppliers can promote their product range more efficiently, and it lowers prices for e-grocery consumers. Everyone involved wins.

The challenge from new business models in the grocery industry is formidable. A combination of new value offerings, operational effectiveness improvements, and promotional innovations from manufacturers can very well give the new model a substantial market share. On the microlevel, if a fifth of total sales went to specialized e-grocers, it would already mean that conventional hypermarkets could not compete anymore and would start going the way of the general store a half century ago.

■ CONCLUSION—NOT ONLY WIN-WIN, ALSO EMERGENCE!

The VOP and OPP are interdependent. Changing your value offering can give you more time to react (time profit), and this also allows you to change your OPP. However, it is not only the VOP and OPP that are linked—we also have links between the value offerings. One plus one is not always two; often it is more, and sometimes less! You need to look not only for individual win-win setups of the demand-supply chain with your customers, but also for links between your offerings.

Consider the basic combination of value offerings proposed for the e-grocery business. Plan and forget is not practical without Don't Run Out, and Don't Run Out is more fun with capture and enjoy. Another example is our nuts and bolts supplier Würth, that leveraged its offer to purchase for small customers to reach a completely new VOP in its OEM customer's aftersales demand chain.

Moving the VOP upstream in the customer demand chain gives you the opportunity to better synchronize to the pace of change of your customer. Dell's offer to planning leverages collaboration on corporate IT standards to manage transitions in its manufacturing and supplier management operations. In the PDA example, collaboration on corporate standards for mobile communication could be used to introduce new products quicker and more effectively to key customer segments.

Evolving tomorrow's business—this is the area where demand-supply chain management can make the biggest difference. The value offering and order penetration points are tools for exploring new opportunities through experimentation and regeneration. Simply being aware of demand beyond the customer order—the options—invites a company to innovate. The primary issue in improving operational performance is not how the supplier can cut cost, or improve current performance. It is, instead, "Can the company reach points earlier in the demand chain of a specific customer, and if not, is there a way to do so by modifying the current operation, maybe moving the OPP, or scaling up a solution developed for another customer?"

Competing in today's business, the company is more likely to find solutions that adapt to customer demand efficiently if he works with demand and supply at the same time. The point is that if the company takes demand and, for example, the offer to purchasing as a given, the assumption is that the customer does not want to change the way he operates. This robs the customer of the opportunity to fully benefit from the relationship with the company, and the company from the opportunity to differentiate.

Innovation is unlikely in an arm's-length relationship regulated by a rigid structure of contracts, purchasing orders, and terms of delivery. On the other hand, assuming that customers may want to operate in a number of different ways, and supporting this with an appropriate mix of value offerings, opens the door to coevolution. The customer can reduce work when the company does more, and the company can streamline its operation, too, because the information available is more reliable.

To keep the customer at arm's length and to keep demand separate from supply may have been fine when information sharing and collaboration were high-cost activities. But as transaction costs drop, the role of the firm, the openness of its borders, and its ability to collaborate must change. So, at this point in time the key to success is collaboration: Suppliers must devise new ways (value offerings) that let the customers improve performance so that the supplier, too, can operate more effectively. And it does not stop there. It is just the start of a process that is capable of transforming whole industries.

■ REFERENCES

1. Miguel Fernandez-Ranada, Xavier Gurrola-Gal, and Enrique Lopez-Tello: "3C—A Proven Alternative to MRP II for Optimizing Supply Chain Performance," Boca Raton, FL: St. Lucie Press, ISBN 1-57444-271-6.
2. Johanna Småros, Jan Holmström, and Vesa Kämäräinen: New Service Opportunities in the e-Grocery Business (forthcoming in the *International Journal of Logistics Management*).

Chapter 6

Operational Effectiveness— Know Your Own Demand Chain

"Know your own demand chain": Make it easy for external and internal suppliers to collaborate with you, which enables you to specialize and focus on developing core competencies.

The key to "getting it" in e-business is to understand your customers' demand chains and use that for value innovation. Companies also have to do their homework, however, and support collaboration and value innovation inside the company and with their own suppliers. The company needs to apply the logic of demand-supply chains on its own operation, as well as on that of its customers. Only then is it possible to build up the complete picture, including process architecture and supporting IT platforms, that the business needs to transform customer performance and achieve operational excellence at the same time.

It is necessary to coordinate material, information, and money flows for efficiency between units within the company and with suppliers. The logic and tools from demand-supply chain management presented in the previous chapters can be applied for collaborating between units and with suppliers as well as with customers. Now the challenge is not to understand your customer's demand chains, but to coach business units and suppliers to make new value offerings to your own demand chains.

Knowing and understanding your own demand chain can help external and internal suppliers integrate and collaborate with you. That way you invite suppliers to develop value innovations that allow you to develop your company's competencies and improve the chain's total performance.

Another important issue is, "How can a company ensure that when trying to serve its customers in multiple ways and collaborating with its suppliers, the result is not one hundred different ways of working inside the company?" The basic trade-off is between process and functional organization. To achieve operational excellence, cost-effectiveness, speed, and flexibility, it is undesirable to build up a multitude of separate end-to-end processes. They make it difficult for a supplier offering a range of products and services to effectively integrate with the company. The compromise is to package and modularize value offerings to customers as well as the collaboration methods with suppliers.

■ ANALYZE YOUR OWN DEMAND CHAIN

The first step in applying the demand-supply chain management approach internally and to suppliers is to analyze and describe your company's demand chains. Analyzing your own demand chain (or, demand chains)—companies usually have more than one) is based on the same simple four-step framework presented in Chapter 2.

➤ Purpose: What Does the Company Do and Why?

A company is organized around many different functions such as production, retailing, aftersales service, product development, and sourcing. Basically, the whole reason for the company's existence is that it is better at fulfilling most of these purposes than more focused specialists. However, the balance between what the company does itself and what it can outsource or use suppliers for changes continually (and given even lower interaction costs, the balance is now moving in favor of outsourcing more and focusing on value innovation). To surf the waves of change, a company first has to develop its sense of balance; it must be in control of its own demand chains.

To use components and material suppliers successfully, you need to grasp the demand chain of a production unit. The easiest way to do this is to analyze one of the company's main end products, or a product family. The obvious purpose in the demand chain of a production unit is to meet customer demand for end products.

However, this is seldom the only demand chain. There are different chains for aftersales replacement parts, and resources to maintain the production unit's capacity to produce. Often the demand chain to support the delivery of end products is well managed and understood. This is why discovering the additional demand chains related to accessories, operations, repair, and maintenance will yield the biggest potentials for value innovations.

➤ Planning: What Is the Demand?

The next step in the demand chain is planning. Although there are several demand chains, serving different purposes, in this illustration we stick to the demand chain for end products.

In a production unit, the demand for components is planned using a bill of materials (BOM) and engineering specifications that define the needed components and their characteristics. Depending on how critical a component is, the specifications may also explicitly state the processes and outside suppliers that can be used.

The BOM, however, is only a standard format for linking end product to component. The critical issue is the demand for the product. This raises a multitude of questions. Is forecasting used to estimate the demand? Who is doing the estimating? What information is used? What are the results of the process? Who uses the results within the organization? How often are numbers updated?

In a typical manufacturing company, planning may proceed in the following way. The first week of every month, the marketing people make a rolling six months' demand forecast by product family, by country, and by month based on historical sales figures and discussions with key account managers. This forecast is consolidated on an Excel sheet, updated by senior sales management, and on the third week of the month it is sent to production units where planners move the first two months' demand figures into the factory ERP (Enterprise Resource Planning) system. Within a week, the updated plans are sent to key suppliers.

Now, what is demand? Because the distribution of planning figures through the company is slow, different parts of the organization as well as the suppliers see demand differently. For the key account, demand is what customers want to buy at the moment, not the estimate discussed with marketing a month earlier. However, for the production unit and the suppliers, this is often the demand information that is used to run the operation.

➤ Consumption: Where and When Is There Consumption?

The reliability of planning inside a company becomes evident when looking at consumption. If there are disruptions or excessive inventory, the planning has not been very successful. To support the production of end products, one solution then is to manage uncertainty by putting in an inventory buffer for components and materials.

When analyzing the fundamentals of materials consumption, we have to go into the details of timing consumption because this is where plans and different ways of managing materials meet. The details that really interest us are the consumption source and procedure for each material item. The issues include how management makes the final decisions on which products to produce and where; how schedules are created, updated, and executed; which phases of the production process require different materials; where to physically locate material inventories; and what principles are used to manage consuming locations.

The focus on consumption may suggest more responsive ways of operating. For example, can consumption be used instead of ordering? Would this enable moving the OPP to a point in the supply chain of the supplier or in the internal production process that makes the company less dependent on detailed level demand plans? Would moving the OPP to assembly eliminate the need to have a forecast for every variant?

➤ Purchasing: How Is the Transaction Made?

The final step in understanding the internal demand chain is to check how demand is actually communicated. For the production unit demand chain for end products, this means analyzing how material needs are consolidated; what kinds of orders are sent to suppliers and how often; what are the requested lot-sizes and delivery times; and where materials are to be delivered. A typical transaction process for a production unit would be a buyer checking materials requirements based on a production plan every week. Based on the plan and how much inventory buffering the production unit wants to do, the buyer makes a purchase order for delivery the next week.

Again, it is essential to understand how the transaction is actually made. In coordinating purchases between many production units and many suppliers, the purchasing transaction—or the inventory count transaction in the case of a VMI solution—is critical. For example, making the daily inventory count closer to consumption improves the benefit of a VMI solution for a supplier.

➤ From Disintegrated Activities to Integrated Demand Chain

After going through and describing one internal demand chain (e.g., the production unit's demand chain for end products), it is easier to do the same with another demand chain. You will find that many phases are the same for different demand chains. For example, the planning stage in the demand chain may be totally different for end products and spare parts but material purchasing is still working the same.

Examining your own demand chain can lead you to many conclusions.

In the best case, your demand chains actually link the production units and key suppliers to sales organizations and channel partners. This indicates that you have been working hard on demand chain management for years and that your demand chain is ready to be opened for value innovations from your suppliers and partners.

In the worst case, you find no links. The sales units and production units are not part of each other's demand chains, and there is no chain linking end-customer demand of a specific product to the production and purchase of materials. This common situation is the result of independent planning processes, consolidations at organizational interfaces, time shifts, internal orders, buffers, and MRP controllers. In this situation, there is much to do inside the company before going further with integration to suppliers.

The stepping-stone for effective collaboration with suppliers is a demand chain from end-customer demand to material requirements. The supplier who is not provided with good quality information will not be any better than the company in synchronizing component supply with demand. Also, the materials consumption and ordering processes of the company have to be expeditious and accurate to support supplier efforts to innovate value in the supply chain.

■ PREPARING THE DEMAND CHAIN FOR SUPPLIER COLLABORATION

How can a manufacturing company provide its suppliers with quality information? The key is how you link the planning-related activities and processes that traditionally have been considered separate—how you link sales forecasting, demand planning, distribution planning, inventory planning, network planning, supply planning, materials planning, and volume planning.

The basic issues are, What do you plan? And, how do you use those plans? The extreme options are that you plan everything you do, on the one hand, or that you plan nothing and respond to everything. The trick is to strike a balance between these positions. The rule of thumb is, "Plan for capacity, execute to demand!" Don't worry about never actually executing the plan; that is not the objective of planning.

This basic rule translates into six principles:

1. Choose planning approach according to your capability to deal with uncertainty.
2. Pace decision making with planning, and execution with feedback.
3. Plan flexibility, not execution.
4. Recognize the product life cycle; plan product introductions and ramp-downs.
5. Use plans to balance supply with demand.
6. Follow up on plans being executed.

➤ Choose a Planning Approach According to Your Capability to Deal with Uncertainty

Because both demand and supply are uncertain, plans are almost without exception inaccurate. The company needs to decide, based on its capabilities, how much emphasis to put on avoiding, reducing, and hedging against uncertainty. Developing a fast and responsive supply chain helps a company avoid uncertainty in demand, but not necessarily in supply. Improving forecasting accuracy also reduces uncertainty in demand. And, inventories can be used to hedge against uncertainty in both supply and demand.

The planning approach depends on both demand and supply. To deal with uncertainty, it needs to be a mix between the different approaches. For example, the company can deliver a line of end products in a make-to-order mode. However, the lead time for some key components is too long for the customer to wait, so forecasting has to be used. And, for some other materials, the supplier is unreliable, so a safety stock is needed.

➤ Pace Decision Making with Planning and Execution with Feedback

Demand is uncertain. This means that a planning process must be dynamic; it needs to receive feedback and prompt decision making.

For both feedback and decision making, a planning calendar makes it possible to update plans and time decisions in a disciplined manner across units and functions. The plan is rolling: The decision-making and data-collecting processes are within a certain interval, and always cover the same time frame. The result is that new plans replace earlier ones.

The important thing to watch out for is that the planning process synchronizes the decision making in the demand-supply chain. All internal functions—sales, distribution, manufacturing, sourcing—as well as customers and suppliers need to make their decisions based on the same situation. The objective is to have "one set of numbers" among all the players, meaning that everybody has the same information on planned demand and supply and will be prepared to meet that.

This requires standardizing data collection and feedback; in addition to a common planning calendar, the players need to have a common definition of products, planning hierarchies, and requirements definitions. Faster feedback can improve execution, or responsiveness, and allows the company to pace execution with daily, or even real-time, performance monitoring and alerts. This, however, does not mean it is planning in real time. Major changes still have to be coordinated and synchronized. The difference is that with more responsive execution, there are fewer situations where players need to synchronize decisions. The result is that the planning cycle to synchronize decisions can be extended, while the feedback cycle is shortened.

➤ Plan Flexibility, Not Execution

One place where the link between faster feedback and less frequent synchronization becomes evident is in capability planning. The company must decide what kind of risks it is ready to take and build up that flexibility in its processes accordingly. The decision on the amount of flexibility capability needed is based on the analysis of forecasting accuracy, nature of demand, and cost of capacity and materials reservations. Flexibility, and not a plan, is then used to execute to actual demand.

Capability needs to be prepared above the demand forecasts; for example, to be ready to deliver variants 25 percent above and total volume 10 percent above a specific sales plan. The tools to build up this flexibility are modular product designs (for mix flexibility), and contract manufacturing capacity (for volume flexibility). Flexibility must be a separate item in planning so that all parties know what the agreed sales plan is and what the agreed flexibility is on top of that. There must also be rules and time lines for how flexibility is used, incrementally consumed or disregarded.

➤ Recognize the Product Life Cycle—Plan Product Introductions and Ramp-Downs

A key issue for a planning process is to manage product life cycles and the dynamics between different life-cycle phases. Managing life cycles requires understanding that different demand chains need to be used in different phases of the life cycle and that demand and supply do not necessarily have to be in balance for the short term.

Especially at successful product introductions, demand exceeds supply. The only issue is how to deal with it in the most profitable way, for both the long and the short term. In the ramp-up phase, supply plans are not necessarily in sync with demand plans as the strategy can be to build a certain ramp-up inventory before starting to sell at all. If there is a strong immediate demand, allocation policies and processes are needed to ensure the most efficient routing of scarce supply when sales start. This process can be strongly supported by collaborating with key customers and focusing on their demand chains.

The formula for effective life-cycle planning is to run it jointly with customers and suppliers so that the shift from one product to another is well managed through the demand-supply chain. This is especially important for those short life-cycle industries where the lead times for key components are extremely long. Therefore, life-cycle planning is a core theme of supplier collaboration.

➤ Use Plans to Balance Supply with Demand

Product introductions and ramp-downs point at the single most important decision in the planning process: how to balance the anticipated demand with available supply and provide feedback on the decision to customers and suppliers. Planning for flexibility and making more decisions responsively reduce the need for balancing, and vice versa.

To do the balancing, we must go through the whole demand-supply chain. We need to do demand planning, supply planning, and demand-supply balancing.

The objective of demand planning is to gather the best possible information on anticipated market demand for the products and formulate that into a demand plan. The demand plan is the input for supply planning. The capacity and materials needed to meet the demand are calculated, with consideration given to inventory positions and possible constraints.

Balancing is a decision-making process for dealing with possible supply constraints. For example, management may decide to prioritize higher margin products and variants when capacity and/or materials are scarce. The trade-off decisions must then be quickly and accurately communicated throughout the demand-supply chain.

➤ Follow-Up on Plans Being Executed

The last principle is a simple management notion. Because the planning process is a core decision-making process, it needs to be followed up. For example, the decision to prepare for a certain product mix flexibility requires that the processes to implement the decision are also put in place.

Following the basic rule of thumb—plan for capacity, execute to demand—and using the preceding simple principles make it easier to reach the goal of a synchronized demand chain inside the company. The next step is realizing a demand chain that is shared with customers and suppliers. We have already discussed collaborative planning with customers in previous chapters and we will get back to collaborative planning with suppliers in the next section. But first, a look at preparing the supply chain for supplier collaboration.

■ PREPARING THE SUPPLY CHAIN FOR SUPPLIER COLLABORATION

If planning process covers the purpose, planning, and managing consumption in the demand chain, the actual demand fulfillment and consumption is on the supply chain side. Analyzing and improving how production and material requirements as well as customer orders are fulfilled can also facilitate supplier collaboration. For example, an integrated, customer order driven fulfillment process inside a company can be extended to the supplier for key components.

When setting up an integrated fulfillment process, you need to pull together several major activities within the company: scheduling the orders, requesting the materials required, making the products, delivering the goods to the customer, as well as paying the bills to suppliers and invoicing and controlling the receivables.

Fulfillment process starts by taking a customer order (or generating an order yourself based on an agreed trigger such as an inventory count) and ends by delivering the requested end product to the customer.

Determining if the order can be delivered is the first area that needs to be prepared for supplier collaboration. Ideally, orders should be confirmed immediately when they are received. A simple procedure is for the company to check whether the product is in stock. For more advanced procedures, supplier collaboration is needed.

In the best case, a company does not have to carry inventory at all but can go all the way to the supplier to check if it is possible to fulfill an order. This, however, assumes that the planning process inside the company is working and the company has capacity to fulfill the order. The better pre-pared the supply chain is, the easier it is to make quick and reliable confirmation checks. This capability to confirm or-ders reliably depends on the supply chain being poised to re-spond to orders and does not necessarily require complex IT. A company and key suppliers that have prepared to fulfill demand with a specific mix flexibility only need to check if total demand is within the limits, and if any exceptions have been flagged.

An important part of preparing the supply chain is lo-cating the order penetration point (OPP). Based on the structure of the product and the speed of the manufacturing process, it is necessary to decide where to locate the OPP and design the complete operational mode around that. The basic options are illustrated in Figure 6.1.

In the buy-to-order mode, the OPP is located at the sup-plier. This means that capacity—but not components, semi-fabricates, nor finished goods—needs to be available. In make-to-order, components need to be ready, as well as capac-ity for manufacturing, assembly, packaging, and shipping. In

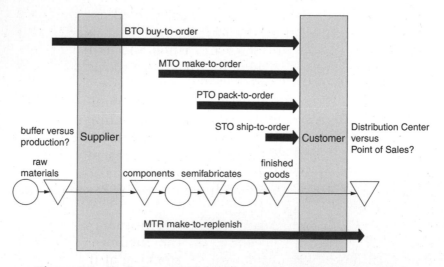

Figure 6.1 Basic Operational Modes Based on the OPP Location

the pack-to-order, the semifinished product and package capacity are needed. And, finally in ship-to-order, only shipping capacity and finished goods inventory are required.

When designing the operational mode, the trade-off is between moving the OPP as far back up the supply chain as possible while still being able to deliver goods as promised. This minimizes the inventory risks and maximizes the capacity and material utilization because goods are only produced against real customer orders; however, customers may have to wait too long. On the other hand, the more advanced the operational mode of the company, the better opportunities for supplier value innovations there are for reducing response times.

Also, once you have identified your OPPs and operational modes, you shouldn't take that as the final configuration. By improving the speed of the execution process and changing the relationship with customers and suppliers, it is possible to increase the degrees of freedom without sacrificing cost or service. For example, the time profit (time profit = the increase in available response time through better information) in replacing orders with inventory count is sometimes enough to move the OPP back all the way to the supplier.

The potential for improving procurement execution with supplier is much simpler for a company that has completed the internal integration of planning and execution. That is because such a company has confirmed and updated plans and actual figures—one set of numbers—for the demand and supply situation.

A basic strategy is for a company to call off all materials with short enough lead times against production orders or replenishment signals. This is commonly known as just-in-time (JIT)-purchasing. Long lead-time items must be ordered against confirmed plans. In addition, based on the chosen flexibility levels, it might be necessary to keep some safety buffers of materials.

Ways to time simplify, reduce, or eliminate non-value-adding activities are speeding up the incoming material flow with more frequent deliveries, stocking at the point of consumption, and developing capabilities to manage small material lot sizes. These also provide great opportunities for value innovation by suppliers. The company, however, must move from discontinuous, consolidated materials administration, toward execution on a real-time basis. Here, the tracking of requirements inside the company operations, buffer status, and immediate goods receipt is critical.

■ THE EXTENDED DEMAND CHAIN—LINK DEMAND TO PRODUCT DEVELOPMENT AND SUPPORT

A final step in preparing a company's own demand chain for supplier collaboration is to extend it on both sides. For a manufacturer, the basic chain—purpose, planning, consumption, purchase—is in most cases an adequate basis for building the demand chain internally.

To get the most value from supplier offerings, however, the basic demand chain is often not adequate on its own. The reason is that many value innovations can be found simply by extending the demand chain and examining how service and product development and aftersales support link into the basic demand chain (see Figure 6.2).

The opportunity is there when, as in many companies, product development and demand-supply chain management are two separate processes that interface only through product specifications. Design for logistics and integrated product ramp-ups are examples of value innovations that are based on bringing the two key processes closer to each other. Design for logistics is essentially an offering that product development can make to production

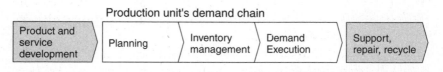

Figure 6.2 Identify Opportunities for Value Innovation by Extending the Demand Chain

and distribution by relaxing constraints on responsiveness and removing cost drivers.

Integrated product ramp-ups, again, is about leveraging the demand chain to support successful new product introductions. To mobilize the demand chain to the support of product introductions, you need to understand how the main phases of a product development process—configuration freeze, supplier and component selection, production ramp-up—change demand. The key variables are reducing supply lead times, improving the accuracy of demand plans, and effectively sharing product specification and ramp-up volume plans between supply chain members.

At the other end of the demand chain for an original equipment manufacturer, new product sales drive demand for support, repair, and recycling services. Often, the demand for these services is such an important part of the business that it is relevant to study aftersales support and spare parts separately as a demand-supply system. This is because aftersales support seldom gets the attention it deserves.

To correct the situation and mobilize supplier support, the company first needs to identify the basic demand chain for the aftersales business by clarifying how purpose, planning, consumption, and purchasing are linked, or can be linked. Practical questions that need answers are how to include spare-parts requirements in the planning process and how to manage the consumption of spare parts. The triggers to start the service delivery processes are especially interesting. The issue is, How proactive can and should the service delivery process be?

Understanding the demand chain for aftersales services is critical if a company decides to outsource all or some of the aftersales delivery processes. The reason is the link between new product delivery and service delivery. For example, spare parts may consume the same supplier capacity as parts for new products.

A company that wants suppliers that innovate new value needs to first understand its own demand and fulfillment processes, as well as how these are linked to product development and support.

■ HELP YOURSELF BY HELPING YOUR SUPPLIERS TO INNOVATE FOR YOU

When a company has identified its own demand chain and prepared its internal planning and execution processes, it is time to open up and invite suppliers in with new value offerings. The objective is to help suppliers make new offerings that enable the company to operate more efficiently or provide its customers with new value. Making it easy for suppliers to collaborate enables the company to specialize and develop its own core competencies.

The logic for working with suppliers is the same as for working with customers. Search for the win-win solutions where suppliers can reduce their costs by offering higher value to the company. In a way, finding value innovations is easier when working with suppliers. A company can greatly improve the odds by how it operates and treats its suppliers. Since it is not a common practice to help suppliers improve their business, but at the same time suppliers commonly use value added and total cost as arguments in their sales and marketing, we have the ingredients for a positive feedback loop. The company points the supplier at a new VOP, and consults the supplier on how to use it to improve its operational efficiency, which in turn motivates the supplier to invest more effort in developing its new capabilities as a standard way to do business.

The way to think about this is that the goal for the company is to be the lead customer for the best suppliers. The role of lead customer entails sharing with those suppliers potential value innovations that the company identifies in its own demand chain. In a successful relationship, the lead customer points the supplier at new business opportunities, while the supplier invests resources in solving the customer's problems.

There are practically unlimited ways that a company can open up its demand chain to suppliers. Figure 6.3 shows a few of the opportunities that the basic demand chain provides, listing some VOPs a supplier could aim at in a manufacturing company. We discuss each of these in turn.

	Purpose	Planning	Consumption	Purchase
Our demand chain activities	Requirements Definition	Demand/ Supply Balancing	Operational Mode, Inventory Management	Demand Execution
Supplier collaboration activities	Life-cycle Management	Collaborative Planning	Vendor-managed Inventory	Streamline Execution
	Road map sharing Collaborative ramp-up/ ramp-down planning Transition planning	Shared forecasts and inventory levels Capacity, flexibility, and liability planning Closed-loop planning	Buffer locations Collaborative inventory planning Replenishment to production Pay on consumption	Eliminating spot orders Eliminating ordering Eliminating nonvalue-adding activities

Figure 6.3   Helping Suppliers Find New VOPs in Your Own Demand Chain

➤ Offer to Purpose: Life-Cycle Management

In manufacturer-component supplier relationships, it is not yet common to talk about product portfolio planning and portfolio management. However, here is a major VOP opportunity related to opening manufacturer product road maps to suppliers. The same way as category management is the basis for new value offerings in the grocery chain, product portfolio management is the basis for collaboration on life-cycle or transition planning, by practicing joint ramp-up and ramp-down planning. Especially if the lead times of components are long, this is the key area to open up for suppliers in short life-cycle industries.

The win win of joint life-cycle planning is that both the company and suppliers can smoothly move from one product generation to the next. The company is able to optimize time-to-market, while both the company and the supplier benefit from better capacity utilization and reduced total inventories and obsolescence.

Joint life-cycle planning is a challenging task as the company opening up to supplier collaboration needs to be able to decide on specific component/supplier combinations across several product families with different life-cycle lengths and technological rate of change. The company also needs to develop the procedures for integrating suppliers with incremental engineering changes in the components and for driving mini ramp-ups and ramp-downs for specific components in the middle of the product life cycles. The benefit is greatest for key components that have customized features, long lead times, high unit costs, or are in scarce supply.

A key activity in joint life-cycle management is the sharing of aggregate volumes for the whole life cycle and detailed collaboration on ramp-up and ramp-down plans. In this process, it is important to discuss and simulate the implications of alternative outcomes. For example, the supplier and manufacturer can commit on equal fixed amounts to produce inventory for the ramp-up, and can determine how to share the risk for obsolescence at the end of the life cycle. Or, the results from analyzing alternative scenarios might prompt a decision to outsource the ramp-down volumes and all the support volumes to a third party to quickly free up capacity for the next product introduction.

► Offer to Planning: Collaborative Planning

Perhaps the most important VOPs to open up for the supplier are offers to planning. Planning collaboration alone can bring significant benefits for both the company and its suppliers by increasing visibility and making supply more responsive. In many cases, planning collaboration is also a prerequisite for the implementation of VOPs in inventory management.

The objective for the company is to help suppliers reserve the right capacity. Whenever possible in collaborative relationships, actual production and delivery also should be based on actual demand, as already discussed. For some long lead-time items, however, it may be necessary to use planning as the trigger to start the supplier's production.

The basis for planning collaboration is that the company has reliable internal planning processes and timely information to share with suppliers. It is necessary for the company that wants to enable offers to planning from its suppliers to develop an introduction procedure. In the introduction, the company explains to the supplier how its planning calendar is set up and what information the plans actually contain. The supplier needs to understand the internal planning process of the company to set up an effective response and to utilize the figures in the supplier's own operation.

Information technology systems can be effectively used to formalize the relationship and deliver timely feedback and new versions of plans. The more mature the company is in its own planning, the more advanced offers the supplier can make in response to flexibility requirements and channel inventories. At this more advanced level in collaborative planning, the issue is not just production volumes. It is also possible to start discussing capacity-based flexibility scenarios and for the supplier to make concrete offers for reserving, billing, and utilizing that flexibility capability to support the company.

An important feature of effective new supplier offerings is feedback. A manufacturing company needs prompt information on how well the supplier can respond to anticipated demand. Just as the feedback information has to be based on execution to support internal planning process, it also needs to be linked to fulfillment in collaborative planning processes. For example, if the supplier can confirm availability, the company can use that as a basis for its own customer order confirmation.

➤ Offer to Inventory Management: Vendor Managed Inventory

In supplier collaboration, perhaps the single most successful concept is vendor managed inventory (VMI) or sometimes even supplier managed inventory (SMI), or jointly managed inventory (JMI). It is an adaptation for the grocery supply chain of the "just-in-time" concept developed by Toyota. Because the VMI approach improves the quality of information passed between a supplier and a customer, it has now been successfully adopted by a wide array of industries in a range of different situations.

An easy access to information on materials inventories and consumption is a first step in prompting more suppliers to implement VMI. An important next step is to discuss with suppliers why inventories are needed, and what kind of availability and service levels the company is looking for to support its own business. For the actual implementation, a prerequisite for success is that the company is prepared to share plans that significantly change demand. Events such as sales campaigns and product mix changes should not come as surprises for the suppliers. The company then can leave it up to suppliers to plan how they will ensure an agreed level of availability and utilize the better information to reduce their own inventory and level their production—to replace inventory with information.

Different trade terms can be used when implementing VMI. Many companies strive toward paying suppliers according to consumption. However, to pressure suppliers that are not yet offering VMI to implement a new process under such terms is counterproductive. Few suppliers are prepared to take the risk before knowing how much the quality of information improves. Additionally, since the successful implementation is based on the company providing information on major changes in the demand, it can be useful if it is the company that owns the inventory.

Only when there is an established collaborative process is it reasonable for a manufacturing company to invite suppliers to make an offer to their production—to take responsibility for physical inventory and let the manufacturer pay according to consumption. This requires suppliers that can take care of availability of materials by the production line based on production schedules and inventory positions. That practically moves the responsibility for materials management to the suppliers and the manufacturer can fully concentrate on its own value-adding production process.

► Offer to Purchase: Streamlining Purchasing

Even if a company is not ready for deeper supplier collaboration changes in the supplier's offer to purchasing can bring significant benefits. For any material that is regularly needed, it may be possible to move away from bundled spot orders (which always come as a surprise to the supplier) to regular weekly or monthly orders that the supplier can more easily forecast.

The key thing a company can do is to provide its suppliers with visibility on future requirements, even though the company still takes care of inventory management and order generation. In response, the suppliers can provide the company with feedback on expected delivery dates, which in turn can be used by the company for its availability to promise.

➤ Configuring the Total Solution: Look as Far Upstream as Possible

Life-cycle management is an enabler for collaborative planning, which is needed for an offer to inventory management to work well. The deeper a company can open up its demand chain, the better opportunities the suppliers have to succeed with a new value offering. The basis for supplier value innovations is set by the company itself. To process is coevolutionary; the successful solution is built on a sequence of win-win solutions.

When repositioning the VOP in the customer demand chain, suppliers can often, by leveraging the better information, also push the OPP backward in their chain. When configuring the overall solution with suppliers, the company may also want to consider the supplier's supplier. In many cases, stocking locations have been reduced and total inventory levels have dramatically declined when manufacturers and suppliers together have designed the new end-to-end solution.

In the electronics industry, building up material management hubs close to manufacturer's site, including some contract manufacturing capabilities, has become a popular form of collaboration. With a hub, the company and its suppliers may immediately replace two separate local inventories (suppliers and manufacturers) with one and move the pull signal from the hub far back into the supplier's production processes. For a customized, high-cost component, an electronic manufacturer used to have 3 to 10 days lead time from the supplier's local warehouse to the manufacturer's factory warehouse. The two stocks were combined in a material management hub, and VMI was set up between the hub and the supplier. The result was direct delivery to the production line and improved availability for the factory. And, for the supplier, the OPP could be moved to its production. The replenishment lead time from the supplier's production to the hub was 7 days.

When selecting possible configurations of VOPs and OPPs with suppliers, the company has to consider several criteria. Do we pursue a single/multiple source strategy? Do we aggregate demand over site and inventory locations? What are the supplier's manufacturing lead time and variation points? What is the variability and commonality of the component in question? What are the availability and flexibility requirements? What is the supplier capacity situation and the life cycle of the material, and naturally what way is the price going? Even though situations change continuously, it is highly important to understand that for the majority of materials and suppliers, the VOP is reviewed only periodically. Once set then, the company uses the most simple solution and processes to support it.

For low-cost, short lead-time, constant consumption items, a company may only want a simple inventory replenishment solution, and no planning collaboration save the addition of new items when introducing new products. Or it may find that some subassemblies can bypass its own inventory management and be delivered directly to the end customer or in transit to the third-party logistics partner.

■ BEYOND ONE-TO-ONE COLLABORATION: SUPPLIER CLASSES AND MODULAR PROCESSES

The better defined the openings for new value offerings are, the easier it is to implement and support them with IT applications. This quickly becomes evident for a company that finds many suppliers are prepared to come up with new innovative value offerings.

Classification is an obvious way to manage a supplier's value offering. In the most simple case, the class defines what type of products the supplier can provide, what the lead time is, and what discounts the supplier gives. However, a company that has opened up its demand chain also needs to classify suppliers based on their VOP and collaboration level (the collaborative planning and fulfillment procedures). The classification can also be expanded to cover important details on the offering like minimum lot sizes, terms of delivery, service levels, and after sales services. In a nutshell, the classification is used to define the supplier value offering from the customer point of view, including the conditions when a supplier can move the OPP.

The classification is essentially a label that facilitates communication with suppliers. At Nokia Mobile Phones, the following classification is the basis for communicating with suppliers: spot order, conventional order, rapid delivery, direct delivery to POS, campaign project, dynamic replenishment (VMI), life-cycle service. An order, or delivery classification indicates that the company itself takes responsibility for what is ordered and when it is delivered. A project, replenishment, or life-cycle label means that a supplier must be prepared to respond directly—without orders—to the company's planning and execution.

For a company, the effective management of supplier offerings requires limiting the number of offerings and developing the capabilities to verify fulfillment for each type of offering. Goods receipt and inspection of the goods is enough to verify an offer to purchase, but an offer to inventory management or planning requires new capabilities. To verify fulfillment of an offer to inventory management, the company needs to start monitoring stock outs and inventory levels by supplier.

After packaging service offerings to customers and suppliers to certain limited VOPs and OPPs, it is necessary to identify the optimized internal processes and capabilities to make these offerings really happen on a daily basis. The service offerings must be matched with the internal demand/supply chain activities analyzed at the beginning of this chapter. At this point, management must make some fundamental decisions on the process architecture.

Many large companies have for years been working on building up global processes and supporting IT systems in different parts of the demand-supply chain. The objective has been tighter integration of sourcing, manufacturing, and distribution by creating a process where before there were only separate functions and business units. This envisioned IT applications architecture is best illustrated as a monolithic, but efficient, process (Figure 6.4).

This one-size-fits-all approach for IT applications does not encourage value innovations from suppliers. One option for the company could be to build up separate processes and flows for each product delivery process, and new value innovation. Although theoretically possible, these highly differentiated processes would be difficult and expensive to build up when going beyond one-to-one collaboration. More importantly, they would be difficult to maintain in the long run. As requirements and offerings evolve, the company and all its suppliers would always have to scrap and rebuild whole processes.

The solution is, that instead of a single standard process or many of differentiated processes, companies can create a modular process architecture by dividing the processes into modular building blocks with standardized interfaces. Suppliers can then make different value offerings by mixing and matching a limited number of process modules provided by the company. The "building blocks" concept is illustrated in Figure 6.5.

The following example from the electronics business illustrates how a modular architecture supports the supplier's value innovation. The new supplier offering is to support the

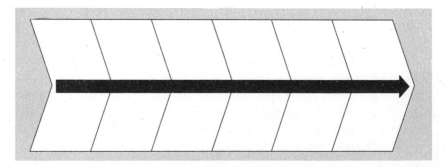

Figure 6.4 Monolithic Process Architecture

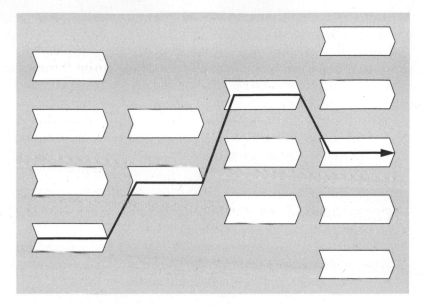

Figure 6.5   Modular Process Architecture

customer company in providing products customized for campaigns—a complex and demanding VOP. In a campaign, customers want customized products for a limited time to promote new applications. The aim is a win-win-win configuration where the customers get the availability of products needed to run the campaign successfully, the manufacturer can assemble these customized products to order, and the supplier gets the demand information early enough to also be in a make-to-order mode. Achieving this new VOP/OPP configuration hinges on a process architecture where the confirmed promotion plan of the customer can be shared with the supplier and serve as the trigger to start production.

Platform thinking and modular applications have gained a strong foothold with software developers. This is important for supplier collaboration because it makes it easier for companies to open up and share applications between organizations. The trend is becoming ever more visible with the introduction of advanced Web toolkits, middle-ware services, and workflow engines.

■ OPENING UP YOUR DEMAND CHAIN FOR INNOVATION IS ORCHESTRATION

As we move away from a world of sequential supply chains to value configurations involving many organizations in different roles, there will be a dramatic shift of power in relationships and the ways to manage suppliers. Also for sourcing, the end customer will increasingly be in the focus.

To help your suppliers serve you better, you need to:

➤ Prepare the demand chain for new supplier offerings.

➤ Actively market the opportunities for new value offerings to the suppliers.

The classification of supplier offerings and a modular application platform are practical approaches to make it easier for the supplier to offer new value to the company. These approaches also make managing variety easier, and responding to new opportunities more flexible.

But more important for encouraging supplier innovations is to simply reveal the demand chain behind the purchase order—open up the options. The primary issue for a company making purchases is not price or how the supplier can incrementally cut costs. Rather, it is: "Can the supplier by reaching points earlier in the demand produce a step change in the performance of the company?"

A manufacturing company can either wait and see what opportunities the supplier develops without active input or become a lead customer for its best suppliers, creating new ways of operating and best practices.

Being a lead customer is another way of looking at orchestration. It means taking an active role in creating opportunities for value innovations—not just sitting back and waiting for suppliers to come with complete offerings developed by and for other companies. This motivates your suppliers to invest in the relationship for their part, and also makes the value offering to the end customer more competitive.

Chapter

Microcosms—Collaborate to Implement Effectively

To implement effectively, you need to include the outside (Implementation = Sell-in + Buy-in).

■ EFFECTIVE IMPLEMENTATION IS THE KEY TO SUCCESS IN DEMAND-SUPPLY CHAIN MANAGEMENT

How to implement effectively is the key success factor in demand-supply chain management. We can't provide a complete guide to effective implementation, because there isn't one. However, we have uncovered important parts of the answer and thus can supply a good "starter's kit" on implementation.

The first, and crucial point, is to understand that selling-in is the key to implementation in the demand-supply chain. This is simply because collaborative business processes go across organizational boundaries, and new solutions have to be "sold," before there can be buy-in and implementation.

When new and more efficient customercentric processes are developed and deployed in business process reengineering projects, only lip service is paid to the insights that marketing, customer relationship, and key account management have about the customer. At the same time, sales and marketing functions continue working with customers undisturbed by operational constraints. The key to successful implementation is integration, not only of supply and demand inside the company but across the whole demand-supply chain.

When we say sales and customer relationship management is the key to effective implementation, we take an outside-in viewpoint. The emphasis is as much on how to implement, as it is on what to implement. Typically product- and production-oriented organizations neglect the issue of how to implement, and concentrate on more exciting "what" questions (e.g., what are the tangible phenomena to address). In doing so, the organizations focus on goals—inventory levels, new value offerings, and collaborative planning processes—and neglect the soft issues (i.e., how to get to them).

But it is the "how" issues that dictate whether a customer is willing to take the risk and to try making changes in practice. In a development effort involving several companies, the success or failure of an initiative is typically not determined by the objectives, but by how implementation is managed and maintained. What seems to make all the difference is the initial deployment and continuous adaptation once the implementation is started.

What is interesting is that the outside-in approach (i.e., starting with the links to the larger whole), also is critical for the success of internal process improvements.

A research team led by Professor Majchrzak[1] at the University of Southern California in Los Angeles, studied 86 electronics manufacturing operations, ranging from production units of large corporations, such as Hewlett-Packard, Texas Instruments, and Unisys, down to small companies. The objective was to find out what factors contribute to success or failure in business process improvement, as measured by lead time. What the researchers discovered is that the following factors enable process improvements:

➤ Process-oriented mind-set, particularly among managers.

➤ Recognition and communication of collective responsibility by management.

➤ Collaborative culture.

➤ Group-based incentives.

➤ Colocation layout.

➤ Jobs with overlapping responsibilities.

➤ Procedures enhancing cross job collaboration.

The common theme of the list is collaboration. A process-oriented mind-set builds on the necessity to collaborate across functions. Collective managerial responsibility, collaborative culture, overlapping responsibilities, group-based incentives, and procedures to enhance collaboration all point toward the conclusion that effective implementation does not need individual heroes, but a collective that can rise above the politics of internal win-lose games.

Maybe the most interesting finding in the list by Majchrzak and Wang, is the factor "jobs with overlapping responsibilities." This is both counterintuitive, and against the practice in most organizations, where clear responsibilities and transparent accountability are believed to lead to results. For implementation, however, the reality is that it is important to encourage risk taking, to just get started, and not to focus only on maintaining efficiency. Overlapping responsibilities promote the sharing of credit for improvements when things go right. But they also motivate individuals to make proactive efforts to prevent problems for colleagues and customers because responsibility also is shared when things go wrong.

Overlapping responsibility is particularly important when implementing new VOP solutions. Hewlett-Packard found this out when transforming the business model toward retailers. As Don Schmickrath,[2] Hewlett-Packard's director of the Product Processes Organization, writes in *Supply Chain Management Review:* "When roles are not rigidly defined, they're very fluid. People see what needs to be done because nobody's doing it, and somebody naturally moves into that space."

For implementations across companies, colocation may initially seem to be an extreme approach. When it is used, however, implementations are often successful. For example, Bosch has colocated some of its engineering department with BMW to implement a collaborative product design and development process. And, Volvo relocated its entire design team for the V80 model, achieving record time to market.

Another example from the high-tech industry is Bose Corporation, a global company that designs and manufactures high-end audio products. Bose has developed and extensively implemented a trademarked business model called JIT II. The essence of JIT II is to bring the supplier into the plant full-time and provide free access to customer data, people, and processes—with an "evergreen" contract and no bidding rituals.

Colocation is just one way to align the interest of players in the demand-supply chain where each has its own incentive system. The issue is not location, but that implementation of radically new business models is difficult before achieving a common view on performance. Therefore, implementation also is difficult as long as group-based incentives are out of reach. And, this is needed to direct cross-company groupings toward a process oriented mind-set building on collaborative culture.

So, if collaboration is pivotal for implementation, then what does the implementation process look like? For implementations across companies, the ideal is a coevolutionary approach. Imagine that a company is actively looking for outsourcing more of its noncore activities. Now, also imagine a supplier is looking for a lead customer for its new value added offering that eliminates the need for many activities on the supplier side. And finally, imagine there is a match between what the company wants to outsource and what the supplier can take more responsibility for. This combination of demand to outsource and drive to develop new value added offerings is the ideal example of a coevolutionary implementation. It is simultaneous buy-in and sell-in from the different companies, driven by a positive feedback loop of win-win situations.

The challenge is to setup implementations in such a way that this can happen. However, it is not about making it happen only once but repeatedly, and with a large number of collaborating companies.

■ MICROCOSMS—COEVOLUTIONARY IMPLEMENTATION WITH ONE COMPANY

First, how do we setup a coevolutionary implementation process with another company?

The key is to include the customer, or the supplier company, as well as your own organization and its functional units. Of course, you do not involve hundreds of people, but just as many as needed to make a microcosm version of the demand-supply chain. A microcosm is a fully operational miniature of the whole business and end-to-end environment to do low-risk and high-speed trial and error.

Bill Hoover[3] and colleagues first presented the microcosms approach in a *McKinsey Quarterly* article in 1996. The background of this approach is the observation that a high proportion of traditional business process reengineering (BPR) projects are abandoned before implementation. To Bill, the difficulty seemed to lie in the way the projects were organized. Once analysis and design were completed, so much time had been wasted that the focus on the common issues had been diluted or lost and sufficient buy-in from all the parties needed for implementation could no longer be secured.

At its simplest, a microcosm is a team brought together across the demand-supply chain, as in Figure 7.1. The microcosm shown in the figure is a European white goods producer, whose French customer was brought in as the key partner to develop and implement new value offerings for the order-delivery process. On the supplier side, two

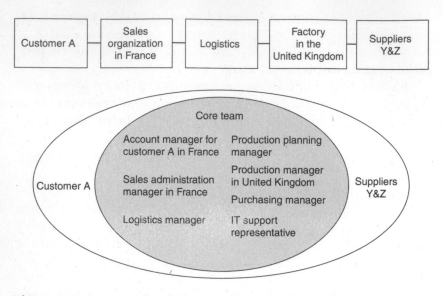

Figure 7.1 An example of a microcosm and its team structure (*Source:* William Hoover et al., *McKinsey Quarterly*)

complementing suppliers were also invited into the microcosm together with the company's U.K. plant.

The team is a composition of the key people involved in the order-delivery process. Ideally, the customer and the supplier would have been full time in the microcosm. In the kickoff stage, however, this was not yet proposed. Instead, key representatives were identified, and their role was to link the company's microcosm to matching supplier-initiated improvement programs.

➤ Move from Shared Information, to Shared Targets, to Implementation

In a microcosm implementation, the critical outside is included in the end-to-end miniature of the business. In this environment, it is possible to work out in practice what is needed to make the coevolutionary implementation happen, to get the positive feedback loop started.

Implementation is a three-stage process (see Figure 7.2). Step 1 is shared information. Step 2 is shared targets (i.e., make the buy-in/sell-in happen). And, Step 3 is shared procedures (i.e., implementation).

Shared information is the first step to setup a coevolutionary implementation process. The key toward success is to focus on opportunities and not just liabilities. Especially in industries where arm's-length relationships are the norm, it is critical to move on from registering and responding to complaints.

Shared information is important to improve the day to day operations of the demand-supply chains. But, let's not make a basic mistake and skip the issue of how to get there. The shared information is most critical in the first discussions of potential joint development initiatives, and in building trust.

Information sharing makes learning possible. In new microcosms, it is necessary to start by collaborating on analysis and conceptualization simply because different members of the microcosm initially do not see the situation in the same way. First of all, the microcosm team needs to establish a common language, which should be specified, communicated, and discussed throughout the participating organizations. But progress should not be dependent on approval and acceptance by each different parent organization.

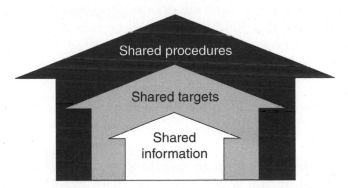

Figure 7.2 Three Steps toward Successful Outside-In Implementation in the Demand-Supply Chain

This task of establishing a common language is far too often neglected in traditional implementations and results in severe implementation problems later. Because different stakeholders lack shared concepts, they misunderstand each other and cannot get a firm grip on the targeted business processes. The parties do not understand what the other tries to sell-in, which leads to a lack of trust and buy-in is not possible. The implementation environment can quickly grind to a complete standstill or turn chaotic as each party makes uncoordinated small changes that cause trouble for the other party.

In the information sharing and analysis phase, it is useful to work on both qualitative and quantitative facts to gain a holistic picture of the state-of-the-art of the process under study. For example, when working with logistics, one has to have a firm understanding of the delivery times and lead times, customer satisfaction, inventory commitment, and cost efficiency. The exact definition of these measures often reveals huge development potential, and improves the buy-in of business process stakeholders, if exposed and communicated to the right levels of the organization.

Shared targets—the sell-in and buy-in of new business process designs—need to be built on the shared insights. This is the next step toward implementation in the microcosm. Sharing information on days of supply and lead times in different stages of the supply chain can often be used effectively to move to shared targets for the process design and performance.

An electronics manufacturer was puzzled by customer dissatisfaction with bad on-time delivery when they started their microcosm program. It turned out that the customer had defined on-time delivery as fulfillment to the request in the customer's warehouse, which was at the level of 60 percent. The manufacturer was convinced it consistently reached 97 percent delivery performance, as was the case when measured against confirmed orders leaving the supplier's shipping dock. In this case, both parties found it straightforward to clear up this misunderstanding, and move on to the next stage in the microcosm. The issue at hand boiled down to "How can the supplier take more responsibility for delivery accuracy and availability in the customer's warehouse?"

Before going into design work in the microcosm, sharing best-practice models can be a shortcut to shared targets and designs. In a microcosm, it is not at all necessary for the company taking the initiative to invent new solution models. It is perfectly in order to build the target design and performance by combining, or scaling up existing solutions. At this stage, the target, or general direction to proceed, needs to be set, but good results can be achieved in various ways.

Truly world-class companies take bigger risks because they may have to experiment with untried business models, but the potential payoff is also greater. However, even the best can learn from analogy, and experiences from different contexts. In a microcosm, it makes sense to quickly make small feasibility studies and get empirical evidence on the applicability of the value innovations from other industries, before committing to target designs. There is always something that every company can learn from any other company. Benchmarking is not an obsolete method for improvements, especially in an environment where ideas can be evaluated and modified quickly.

Once a shared target is found inside the microcosm, the next step is sell-in and buy-in from the organizations and functions where change may become necessary. Far too often, the companies are in too great a hurry to implement a new "neat" concept. This is a mistake and partly explains why many re-engineering projects fail. The basis for coevolutionary implementation is to develop a clear value offering that can be sold-in, to the appropriate points in the customer demand chain. The odds for successful implementation improve manifold once the drive to sell-in is matched by buy-in.

After making the sell-in and buy-in match, the next step is implementing the shared procedures. The target blueprint for each shared procedure needs to be decomposed into its key elements, and the implementation milestones defined to make the actual steps manageable. This phasing approach makes it possible to build in trial-and-error loops, and to co-ordinate implementation with training and competence development. (Training and competence development is a cornerstone for extending the individual microcosm to the program and will be discussed later.)

Writing up blueprints and subjecting them to conceptual and pre-operational validations is part of the sell-in process. However, process simulations, computer models, and simulation games can be a more useful way to package the blueprint. A model can be transferred and reused in new microcosms more easily than a document to rapidly build up a shared target. Yet, by far the most important validation source is piloting in the microcosm with the customer and/or the supplier.

The implementation—from a single customer perspective—is complete when the pilot developed in the microcosm is tested and validated in practice. However, for the company developing a new value offering, implementation is only starting. The process, from information sharing and building the shared target to implementation, needs to be packaged and incorporated in IT systems and business processes of the company as a whole.

When working with the coevolutionary, microcosm approach, the distance from concept to real-life validation is short. Decomposing difficult, large problems vertically into customercentric analysis—design—implementation sequences is a novel action-oriented approach that only a few companies have mastered. The challenge is how to set up the right microcosm.

➤ Setting Up the Microcosm — Value Innovation with the Right Constraints

The microcosm speeds up value innovation and implementation. But, how do you set up the microcosm to provide constraints in the implementation process that produce relevant results in the full-scale business? What are the constraints to take account of, and where to start?

Setting up a microcosm creates an environment that supports coevolutionary target setting and implementation.

Reducing the scale and number of constraints creates the right environment. For example, a microcosm can be built up by focusing on a particular customer, a single product or product family, part of a plant, and the supplier of a key component of these integrated pilots. This end-to-end slice provides the common focus and platform for information sharing, target setting, and implementing shared procedures.

The important decisions in creating a microcosm involve the product, the customer, and production and distribution organizations. Of these, however, the key decision is selecting the right outside partners—the customers and suppliers—to invite to work in the microcosm. The criteria to apply for selection are:

➤ Opportunity for value innovation.
➤ Business relevance and potential to scale up value innovations.
➤ Access to key decision makers and implementers.

The opportunity for value innovation is the primary concern. Setting up microcosms with customers in segments where advanced value offerings have already been developed and deployed is less important than initiating the coevolutionary process in segments where few value innovations have been made. The opportunity is typically the greatest where there are the most problems.

It is critical to remember the order-less business models, or to check what comes before the order in the demand chain. Far too often, the new partners in a microcosm jump directly to solving current issues in the execution of the order-delivery process, without considering the opportunities to eliminate parts of the process through closer collaboration. For example, rather than focusing on delivery lead times, sharing information on sales plans and inventories can be the basis for reaching for a new VOP in inventory management or collaborative sales promotions.

The second point is business relevance and potential to scale up value innovations. When picking a customer with whom to set up a microcosm, the customer's current size and growth potential are obviously relevant criteria. Simply put, the effort may quickly become an important source of new revenue and profit if the right customer can be involved. But, this is only part of the story. Maybe even more important is the potential to expand a new value innovation to many more customers. This means a selection criterion should be that the customer belongs to a larger group that can benefit from a new solution. If the microcosm customer turns out to be unique regarding its targets and required solutions, it is necessary to repeat the whole exercise when the company wants to improve its value offering to another customer.

Access to the customer's decision makers and implementers is an indication of both the willingness and capability of the customer to develop collaborative business models. A precondition is the willingness of the account and category management to participate in the microcosm. Account and category management fulfill a gatekeeper role in sales and purchasing respectively, and thus provide—or prevent—access to the key people needed for implementing collaborative business processes. An issue in the relationship between large organizations is that the gatekeepers on both sides often see their role as protecting their own organization or their customer from interference and distractions. The downside is that even though the commercial relationship may be close and long term, the collaboration does not reach the operational levels, and the opportunities for value innovations are diminished.

■ MICROCOSM PROGRAM—COEVOLUTIONARY IMPLEMENTATION WITH MANY COMPANIES

The challenge is to set up coevolutionary implementation not just once but repeatedly and with a large number of collaborating companies. It is necessary to organize a microcosm program to initiate and support coevolutionary implementation with many partners.

To achieve differentiation and integration at the same time is a complex task. You must differentiate the value

HEWLETT-PACKARD'S DaVINCI PROGRAM

Hewlett-Packard discovered the coevolutionary improvement approach in the early 1990s as they fought to solve order-fulfillment problems hampering the company's ability to deliver products. Don Schmickrath,[4] director of the Product Processes Organization, describes in his article "How Do Caterpillars Learn to Fly," in *Supply Chain Management Review,* how the evolutionary, modular, and iterative approach to invent and implement effective business models and processes was discovered through trial-and error learning.

In 1991 HP had started a major development effort—a program called "Tornado"—to address the problems in order fulfillment. After $2^{1}/_{2}$ years of labor-extensive and costly efforts, the project was canceled.

But Hewlett-Packard did not give up. The company launched a radically different approach that became the DaVinci project. The DaVinci team proceeded to run a series of pilot programs and bring different businesses onto an integrated value offering platform in an iterative fashion. The objective is to differentiate offerings by customer and product lines (from printers to personal computers) but at the same time integrate the solutions and implementation approach across retail, commercial, and consumer segments.

How is the differentiation achieved? The mechanism to develop new value innovations collaboratively with different customers is to organize the work as a sequence of "narrow, deep slice" pilots bringing the customers and suppliers of the company to work together with HP's internal production and distribution organizations. In the case of the order fulfillment process, HP started with a single customer (United Stationers, a reseller) and a single product family (Laserjet Toner) in the computer supplies business. The successful implementation was followed by a sequence of new implementations selling-in and enhancing the new value offerings on the way.

(continued)

HEWLETT-PACKARD'S DAVINCI PROGRAM (CONTINUED)

But, how can integration be achieved at the same time? To integrate implementation and business use as well, as solutions in the DaVinci program, Hewlett-Packard follows a simple set of principles that they call the "6000 rule." The acronym "6000 rule" stands for four principles for business process development projects:

1. The "6" stands for "getting measurable business results in six months." Don Schmickrath emphasizes, "Large projects accomplished in a monumental 'big bang' (no matter how long that might take) are a thing of the past." To get results in six months, it is necessary to divide implementation into smaller, manageable business projects, where fast results are achievable and feedback can be received on both the customer's benefits and on necessary improvements before expanding to new customers.

2. The first "0" *stands for "Zero Risk."* Piloting on a small scale should not in any way risk or harm the rest of the business. It is of paramount importance to avoid hurting the company or its partners when implementing new collaborative processes. The focus on smaller, manageable six-month business implementations, including the piloting and learning from iterations, helps reduce risk.

3. The next "0" refers to the information systems part of integration, and stands for "Zero Changes to Code." HP has observed that although customers and internal players are keen to propose changes in the IT tools used in the demand-supply chain, the different units also have a hard time taking benefits out of modifications. The basic reason is the inclination to overdesign to deal with situations that hardly ever occur in practice coupled with the high cost to deploy the changes in the IT tools.

HEWLETT-PACKARD'S DAVINCI PROGRAM (CONTINUED)

4. The last "0" stands for "Zero Interfaces." Integration between the company and a growing number of collaborating partners is easier to maintain and increase when old systems and solutions can be killed off. The implication is that when moving to a new integrated software solution, the interfaces to the existing IT systems should be minimized. If the proper discipline cannot be maintained, more and more resources are required to maintain and operate the systems solutions.

On the surface, HP's implementation approach and 6000 rule seem simple, but to achieve the same level of effectiveness in implementation requires a deeper understanding of organizational requirements.

offerings to the customers, and how you work with your suppliers. At the same time, you must integrate the solutions and procedures (create a platform) and integrate implementation with business use (set up a program, or a permanent process to capture new opportunities and transfer value innovations to larger parts of the business).

Setting up and deploying a coevolutionary implementation process can be divided into three phases: initiative and kickoff, learning and selection, and program alignment and launch.

1. *Initiative and kick off.* The company identifies the opportunity, commits resources, and outlines the program from initiative to alignment and launch.

2. *Learning and selection.* The company first must learn in practice how to get coevolutionary implementation going with one, or a very small number of partners, as well as select one or more of the developed new value offerings for large-scale implementation in a program.

3. *Program alignment and launch.* Here, all the necessary organizational and new implementation processes can finally be aligned with each other and the program is launched.

➤ Initiative and Kickoff—Setting Out in the Right Direction

Recognizing the opportunities in demand-supply chain management is the basis for aspiring to acquire the skills needed for coevolutionary implementation with a larger number of partners. For example, the initiative can come from a successful individual implementation case, or be the result of a systematic identification of value innovation opportunities in the demand-supply chain of the company. However, it is crucial to realize that the program has to be created through practice and carefully molded from the collaborative work in individual microcosms.

You do not need to start implementation from scratch. Before kicking off the first microcosms, it is useful to have a rough blueprint, defining the target, potential solutions, or benchmark examples, and the potential scale for the business opportunity.

You can start by identifying the demand chains and potential VOPs for key customers in your different business segments, or in the businesses of your customer's customer. A consumer electronics producer might start with customers in its main business segments:

➤ Mass merchandisers (e.g., Wal-Mart).
➤ Warehouse stores (e.g., Sam's Club).
➤ Department stores (e.g., Sears).
➤ Mail and telephone order companies.
➤ Original equipment manufacturers (e.g., a carmaker).
➤ E-tailers.

Partner companies in different segments, or channels, add value differently. The company could relatively easily become an e-tailer itself, or offer a "shop-in-shop" to e-tailers. But the company could not, without the collaboration of car manufacturers, sell factory-installed car stereos to consumers buying a new car. The important point is not to get stuck here. The key is to find a "good enough" opportunity for a first microcosm, not the best possible.

The issues addressed in the blueprint so far have been the same considerations as needed for launching an individual microcosm. However, there is a difference. In the blueprint—when aiming for a program—you also need to address resources, competence building, and integration issues. These do not need to be resolved yet, but the goal of acquiring the competence to replicate and scale up coevolutionary implementation processes must be clearly stated, and the outline of the program defined.

The key decision is to commit the necessary resources to "grow" individual microcosms into a full-fledged microcosm program. In addition to the microcosms, resources are needed to:

➤ Support microcosms in developing both short-term wraparound IT solutions and in finding the necessary integrated solutions.

➤ Develop training programs and collect best-practice experience.

➤ Support the identification and kickoff of new microcosms.

Support for wraparound solutions is particularly important in large corporations, as is support in finding solutions that use existing systems. Providing data on inventories in the channel, and even at the point of sale is often difficult. If neither party has the tools available, the simplest best option to share an existing system is not available! In such a situation, the second or third best alternatives have to be found. In a microcosm between a telecommunications company and an operator, the lack of a tool to share inventory levels could be solved without delay by creating a simple

Lotus Notes application. This would be possible because the need to provide supporting wraparounds was anticipated.

The second important point is securing resources for developing training and synthesizing experiences. Overcoming competence gaps is a severe problem when a company wants to move from individual microcosms to a microcosm program. The competence development programs need to be designed, tested, and launched in parallel with the actual coevolutionary implementation process.

Therefore, it is important to include competence development experts in the field from the beginning. Initially, the same persons responsible for developing training and best-practice solutions can also support the setup and kick-off of new microcosms. When the scale increases, however, support also needs more resources.

Simulations and mockups are good tools for both training and disseminating best practices. The danger is that conceptual models are easily misunderstood. A working, live specification—a simulation model, prototype, or mockup—is a tangible platform for discussion that is much more easily understood.

It is important to plan ahead. Training, resources, and support processes are the cornerstones for creating an organization and a way to work that can reproduce coevolutionary implementation with customers, renew the solutions and implementation with customers, and regenerate the whole program after launch.

➤ Learning and Selection—Practice before Organization

The first phase, initiative and kickoff is followed by a phase of the learning and selection in practice (i.e., the first, or first few microcosms). Only after these inductive, empirical exercises with different key customers and suppliers are new value innovations adequately conceptualized and ready to be communicated. They are then ready to be packaged for sell-in and coevolutionary implementation with a larger group of partner organizations.

The open-ended search for value innovation in cooperation with selected outsiders is uncomfortable for companies with a traditional closed corporate culture. Although the decision on whom to approach is carefully prepared in the microcosm plan, traditional organizations still prefer to design first and then decide which customers and suppliers to approach. We are challenging this order. The underlying argument is simple: If the designs for new collaborative business models are frozen before testing and development with real customers, it is just by pure chance that any design actually is a value innovation for the customer.

This mismatch between sell-in and buy-in is a root cause of spectacular failures in reengineering projects. Even if requirements and processes are thoroughly analyzed, it is still only by chance that a design addresses both the customer's real needs and constraints to efficiency. The risk is overengineering and inflexibility. The initial design freezes the degrees of freedom. When new opportunities are identified while working with the customer, these are difficult to accommodate because the initial design has already established the mind-set of the design team.

The two approaches can be illustrated as follows:

1. The traditional approach would be to develop a ready solution, and then approach the first customer with the proposal: "We are here to help you get our goods with a shorter order fulfillment lead time." However, order fulfillment lead time might not be a problem at all. The problem may be that some orders are not fulfilled at all, and the customer feels that the supplier does not give a damn about the damage it causes the customer's business. This is not a very good start for closer collaboration.

2. The alternative approach would be to propose sharing information with the customer to get an understanding on what disruptions cause the biggest problems, and where improvements are most urgently needed. This avenue can be much more effective. Above all,

the supplier gets a better understanding of how the customer operates, which is essential for value innovation.

After having pointed out that it is critical to develop new value innovations collaboratively, we must take a step back. How do we ensure that the new value offerings can be integrated with existing processes and that they can also be used with other customers, or suppliers? The tool for this is a blueprint that is specific enough to serve as an entry point to collaboration, but open enough to serve as the basis for a value innovation. The challenge is to have a rough outline that highlights the high-priority or high-potential issues, which can then be built on in the microcosm. As the work proceeds, it is essential to document not only the solution design, but also the information sharing and target setting.

Prior to the practical implementation of each microcosm, the blueprint is adjusted to provide best support for IT, training, and work in microcosms. Also, after each microcosm implementation, there is a wrap-up workshop to evaluate and improve both the "what" and "how" of the new collaborative business process.

After using this iterative design and development of both solutions and implementation for the first few microcosms, the company has both:

➤ Tested and tried value innovations (i.e., real-life business cases).

➤ The blueprint for building the needed organization and skills to roll out the value innovation to many potential customers.

The company knows how to set up a coevolutionary implementation, how to set itself up for sell-in to a point in the customer demand chain where there is good opportunity for buy-in. The challenge at the end of the learning and selection phase is to make a step-change in scale, and start replicating the successful new solutions and implementation process across product lines and business units.

➤ Program Alignment and Launch—Organization for Differentiation and Integration

To make a step change in scale requires a completely different mind-set from setting up and running a few individual microcosms. In the learning and selection phase, the typical number of customers involved can be expressed with a single-digit number. In the program alignment and launch phase, the ambition level is to reach tens, if not hundreds of business partners with the new offering and the associated implementation approach.

To make the step change, you need to integrate what is offered with how it is implemented. The objective of the microcosm program is to develop an organization that can integrate while increasing differentiation; it can improve efficiency while value innovating. The components that need to be aligned with the coevolutionary implementation approach before launching the program are:

➤ The solution and sell-in platforms.
➤ Training and support resources.
➤ The ownership of the program.

A solution platform is the tool to integrate business processes that have been allowed to develop divergently. Most companies today already have solution platforms. As the Hewlett-Packard case suggests, leveraging existing systems can reach a long way.

Many companies have problems using their existing IT systems to differentiate their value offerings not only because of the inflexibility of the systems, but because of their management of master data. Master data can be a powerful tool to manage process variants (i.e., to customize processes while increasing the standardization of operations).

Imagine a company that has 1,000 customers and plans to design and implement customized business solutions for each customer individually! The costs to set up and maintain such a huge variety of business processes would be astronomical. Working in hundreds to thousands of business process variants simultaneously would make life impossible for the operations people (production, warehousing, shipping, configuration, etc.) not to mention the problems of providing necessary IT support. In all, convergence to just a few process variants is a must.

To leverage parameters as mechanism for differentiation, the key skill to learn is the use of customer master data and product master data management. Differentiation can be achieved with a particular customer by adjusting master data parameters while leaving the structure and basic conditions of the processes intact. The issue is not to choose between differentiation and no differentiation, but between standardization and no standardization. Converging the different processes on using standard operations and controlling these with standard variables can simplify the task of increasing differentiation and integration at the same time, and make it achievable.

Platforms and modularity are today an almost self-evident feature for business process solutions. Not only the solution, however, but also the implementation requires a platform. To make the step change, setting up the coevolutionary implementation environment also needs support and a platform. Although a platform to support information sharing, developing shared targets, and setting up shared procedures and solutions may not have existed before in the company, it can be developed based on the first microcosms.

A mix of offerings—a solution platform that can be customized—is a must because the company will never be able to sell-in the same advanced new offerings to all its customers at the same time. However, for sell-in support, self-service is the objective. This means that an important part of the sell-in platform is a road map and a follow-up system, maybe in the form of a partner program. Ideally, using these aids, the partners can serve themselves to more advanced value offerings as time goes by. With a well-thought-out program and implementation road map, the steps toward a full-blown collaborative business model become more manageable.

Platforms and IT support are critical for converging different value offerings onto the same solution modules, but the business side is just as important. The business side needs to understand its role in the value capture process, and to acquire this knowledge, training and communicating best-practice experiences are equally critical.

The second point that needs to be aligned with the implementation approach is training and support. The successes from the previous phase need to be replicated. We are not talking about two to three more experiments but a sequence of rolling out value innovations by selling-in to tens, maybe hundreds of customers and/or suppliers. A global company definitely needs a longer time to align and launch the coevolutionary implementation approach than a smaller domestic player. But in any case, training and competence building are key factors that have to be aligned before a successful launch. An issue with regard to training and competence building is how to reach outsiders? For work in a microcosm, it may be necessary to train customer or supplier representatives before even attempting to begin the information-sharing activities.

The training and competence building also plays an important role for renewal and regeneration. This is how feedback on new best practices can be effectively passed between different players in large organizations and serve as the trigger to go back and search for new opportunities.

Implementing value innovations is a major learning process. Initially, there are major competence gaps in the line organization. But as practical experiences accumulate, the best experts for training and competence building can be found in the line organization. It is important to mobilize this expertise when making the step-change.

The third part of the alignment to get right is the ownership of the program. The ownership for differentiation falls naturally with customer and supplier management, however the ownership for the coevolutionary implementation approach is often overlooked. For alignment and a successful launch, the approach—the how to do it—needs nurturing from the top. Leadership, not just support, is needed.

■ BIRD PROGRAM—ALIGNING SYSTEMS, RESOURCES, AND LEADERSHIP FOR COLLABORATION

Nokia, a pioneer in the mobile telecommunications industry, was among the first to enter the business in the 1980s. Since those days, demand for cellular telecommunications has skyrocketed, and today the company is the number one producer of handsets, and the number three supplier of network infrastructure.

To improve customer satisfaction and reduce the lead times throughout the chain, Nokia Networks (Nokia's division to design, manufacture, and market telecom infrastructure, such as digital cellular networks) launched a collaborative development program, called the Hand Shake (HS) project, together with its key customers, the operators.

What the company found was that customers' demand chains differ greatly. Some operators are entrants, others incumbents, and the way they purchase and deploy digital cellular networks differs depending on their core competencies and business strategies. An established operator may be expanding by building a network in a new market, but may also be improving customer service by building on existing networks. Operators in a new market or new entrants in an existing market, focus solely on network building. Some of the operators, particularly among incumbents, prefer turnkey solutions. They are highly conscious about their core competencies and therefore, outsource network planning and installation, to knowledgeable partners.

The demand-supply chain for building and upgrading cellular telecommunications infrastructure is complicated. The operator's purpose for building and upgrading a wireless telecommunications network is acquiring a revenue machine. The primary role of the telecom equipment company is to produce and deliver the necessary packages of hardware and software.

Because the operator provides the consumer with mobile communications services, the infrastructure is installed on sites throughout the terrain wherever the consumers move and want to communicate, from the city to the tops of the mountains. The site acquisition activity is fundamentally important for the operator, because consumers' satisfaction is highly dependent on availability of the network for the consumers. The availability is based on network coverage and capacity, which are factors strongly related to the number, location, and capacity of the base station sites. Site building is construction work, regulated by local laws, municipal directives, property ownership, and so on. The basic demand-supply chain for telecom equipment is shown in Figure 7.3.

The problem for the equipment supplier is the lack of shared processes with the operator. In the best case, the operator places the final order only when the site is ready; and as the telecom network is the operator's revenue machine and the license fees in many countries are high, the operator also insists on a very short order fulfillment lead time. The complication with ordering in advance is that it is necessary to check the status of the building permission, civil engineering, power supply, and installation teams before shipping anything to the site.

There does not seem to be a single business model between the telecom operator and the technology supplier. Operators insist on short time-to-revenue creation that implies

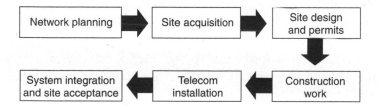

Figure 7.3 The Basic Demand-Supply Chain for Telecom Equipment

to short order fulfillment lead time needs. On the other hand, the site should be ready regarding both timing and content prior to any equipment being forwarded to the site. For timing, it is necessary to have all the site related preconditions met before any delivery is worthwhile. For content, the final configuration needs to be known in details. And, above all this complexity, the sites of cellular networks are interrelated: A base station configuration of a site may affect the configuration of the neighboring cells. But, as speed was so important, the solution had been to build a network of distribution warehouses that could serve the operators on short notice. This is very expensive, because it distributes large amounts of high-tech equipment to many locations. As some of the equipment is even configured to operator specifications, the obsolescence risks are high, as are the risks for price erosion.

➤ Initiative and Kickoff

In the Hand Shake program, Nokia and its customers learned that the way to sort out the challenges was to increase collaboration in demand/supply chain management. Better alternatives for both the operator and supplier exist, as the Hand Shake project had shown. Through the collaborative development program, Nokia learned that there is no single optimal business model even for an individual telecom operator. Instead, depending on the situation—the demand chains—there were a set of preferred business models for the telecom operator, each applicable in a particular situation. The company had to learn the skills of developing differentiated, but yet integrated demand-supply chains together with its customers.

The response was to initiate and set up a new collaborative business model development and implementation program, called BIRD. The key idea of BIRD was to vary Nokia's value offering depending on customer's demand characteristics and business situation. Another peculiarity was the learning oriented collaborative development approach. The open-ended coevolutionary approach promised to simultaneously increase the offering and improve operational effectiveness.

Mr. Eero Virros, Director, Deployment Programs at Nokia Networks, described the program's objectives: "Faster time to profits for the customers, value innovation, and cost and productivity leadership for the supplier." There was also a strategic objective, to acquire the capability to deploy new demand-supply chain solutions and best-in-class processes in collaboration with customers. Similarly to the earlier HS program, the focus of the BIRD program still was in the volume part of the wireless telecommunication network, for example, the base station network.

A rough blueprint was made based on the insights from the Hand Shake projects. For the supply chain, three alternatives were identified depending on the OPP:

1. Country warehouse (current solution).
2. Regional distribution center.
3. Direct delivery from the factory.

On the demand side, three alternatives could also be found for the basic value offering:

1. Box delivery (base station deliveries and alike standard technology delivered as equipment only).
2. Telecom deployment (supplier responsible for equipment installation and integration to the network).
3. Turnkey (complete turnkey solutions for the operators).

For identifying and setting up microcosms, three basic dimensions were used: the customer, product, and potential business model. Based on the presumed variations in customer requirements and the products, the open agenda microcosm-like approach sounded far better than the uniform waterfall model to make the appropriate choice for the business model.

➤ Learning and Selection—Practice before Organization

The first microcosms in the BIRD program were set up to validate and improve on the rough blueprint with real-life implementations together with customers. It was also valuable to identify the necessary competence and IT support requirements in an explicit form. These requirements were simply based on the experiences gained with the first microcosm solutions. However, the learning of all the others was the approach to create and deploy a new business process end-to-end with key customers. The work in the microcosms proceeded from information sharing, to setting common targets, to implementation.

The collaboration was sold-in with different arguments depending on the situation, but the "fastest time to profits for customer" proved effective for a range of situations. This target setting shifts emphasis from order fulfillment to the total lead times until the customer can turn the network on and start to sell airtime to its customers. Internally, between Nokia organizational units, the potential for tangible asset reduction was an effective target to align interests.

Instead of focusing merely on the call-off lead times for the deliveries from Nokia, it was possible to start implementing shared processes for reaching demand before call-offs. Access to the operators' network construction plans, site acquisitions, construction permissions, civil engineering work, and availability of installation teams proved to be a foundation for designing and implementing new value offerings. For Nokia, reaching earlier in the demand chain enabled moving the OPP, reducing inventory, and improving on-time delivery as the planning accuracy improved.

The collaborative planning and forecasting processes between Nokia and its customers varied a lot, as did the supply chain solutions. To converge the implementations, a basic rule was formulated: "Plan for capacity—execute to order!" The cornerstone for the platform is using the operator's plan. Naturally, it is never 100 percent accurate, but it is the only one on which any judgments and preparations can be based. Therefore, the other part of the platform solution has to support executing to order in different circumstances. It must trigger the correct order with delivery content, timing, and destination—with or without a formal customer order—from different points in the demand chains.

A significant part of the solution platform is synchronizing the demand chain with the supply chain. In practice, this means that the same monthly pace for collaborating with the customer is used also in the internal planning. The unified metrics to monitor delivery performance is also an important element in the platform building.

However, more critical than establishing the solution platform was learning how to set up a successful coevolutionary implementation. Identifying the offer of "fastest time to profits for customer" was the key for getting operator buy-in for collaborative processes.

A standard five-step format, with milestones and time lines, was formulated for the work in microcosms. The target was, as in the DaVinci example, to get results in less than half a year. One month is reserved for preparation and information sharing to set the common target, three for the actual design and implementation work and the last one to three months for the follow-up (see Figure 7.4).

Another important practice stressed by Mr. Virros is that before setting-up a microcosm, any potential contractual implications must be reviewed and settled with the customer. The bottom-up implementation with partners operating in complex multilayered organizations requires having such contract terms that enable streamlined process utilization in

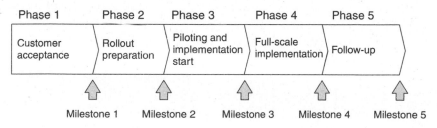

Figure 7.4 Microcosms in a Standard Five-Step Format

practice. This lesson stems from experiences when the front-line customer representatives looked forward to implementation after successful design work in a microcosm, but permission to proceed was denied because contracts specified the following of other working practices.

Perhaps the most important task in the learning and selection phase is to document success. Building on success makes selling-in easier with every new customer. This was also exactly what happened with the BIRD program. The implementation work in the BIRD program with 24 customer accounts in 18 months was a major contributor to the overall 39 percent reduction in inventory days of supply in Nokia Networks. And, inside Nokia, the reduction of inventories in the new demand-supply chain was a strong argument for scaling up the new implementation approach to the next phase.

➤ Program Alignment for Replication

Critical for program alignment and launch is establishing ownership for both the differentiated solutions and the implementation approach. For the differentiated solution strategy, the key is to reach the key persons from Nokia's account teams and their counterparts in the customer organization. But for the implementation approach, it is critical to include demand-supply chain management, project management, and information management from Nokia's country and regional organization.

The BIRD program offers value thresholds for the customers. The foremost of them was expressed as "fasted time to profits for customer." This target setting emphasizes the total lead times until the customer can turn the network on. Besides the reduction of the delivery times, the delivery reliability improved essentially.

Additionally, the generic business processes created as the by-product of the BIRD program provides a sufficient degree of configuration flexibility depending on the customer and the market situation. The best demand/supply chain configuration is designed for each particular business relationship.

Besides the order fulfillment lead times, the extended collaboration has brought up other joint targets. Sharing more information, the preconditions for flawless execution have been improved. The earlier mainstream solution to serve the customers from the country warehouses amplified the expectations for short lead times. However, as most of the configurations are customized, short order fulfillment lead times had been quoted on the cost of on-time delivery. This was a dilemma. The mainstream BIRD solution is a delivery directly from a factory or from a regional distribution center, which ensures a more reliable perfect-order-fulfillment (on-time, complete, perfect quality).

The role and activities of logistics service providers have also been redefined in preparation for expanding the coevolutionary implementation approach to new business areas and regions. The transportation and forwarding processes and flows have been standardized, and the role of the logistics services companies as partners has been revitalized and expanded. This has reduced the number of players in logistics activities while the value added from their side as a whole has increased. This also makes it easier to copy best practice implementation processes, and scale up successful solutions.

The BIRD program can definitely be considered a success by any measure. Improving demand/supply chain management is a never ending crusade and BIRD still continues. Eero Virros and his team have moved the reality a step closer to the vision. Interestingly, Mr. Virros does not consider the tangible result performance as the best result of BIRD. He emphasized the leverage of improvement is process performance and the way they are made. Nokia has learned, together with its customers, to collaboratively discover new solutions over and over again.

■ REFERENCES

1. A. Majchrzak and Q. Wang, "Breaking the Functional Mind Set in Functional Organisations," *Harvard Business Review,* September–October 1996, 93–99.

2. Don Schmickrath, "How Do Caterpillars Learn to Fly—Transforming Supply Chains at Hewlett-Packard," *Supply Chain Management Review,* Winter 2000, 22–32.

3. William E. Hoover Jr., Magnus Tyreman, Joakim Westh, and Lars Wollung, "Order to Payment," *McKinsey Quarterly,* No. 1, 1996, 38–49.

4. Don Schmickrath, "How Do Caterpillars Learn to Fly—Transforming Supply Chains at Hewlett-Packard," *Supply Chain Management Review,* Winter 2000, 22–32.

Chapter

Managing Information Technology—How to Stretch Your Business to Its Full Potential

Technology not only is an enabler, but also is setting limits for value innovations.

■ INFORMATION TECHNOLOGY SETS LIMITS ON YOUR BUSINESS OPERATIONS

In the evolution of demand-supply chain management, information technology enables companies to integrate activities and organizations that before were separate. Or, to put it another way: Technology sets limits on what you can efficiently manage on the operational level.

In the 1970s when many companies started applying IT, automating functions was their upper limit. The first IT applications developed to improve operations were order taking, inventory management, and billing systems. The goal was to reduce the costs of data processing in individual functions, but it quickly became obvious that significant improvements in efficiency could be achieved by linking the functional systems.

For example, companies could process more inventory movements and more reliably if they linked the order-taking system to the inventory management system. However, the links were batch interfaces, and as a consequence work progressed slowly from function to function, albeit automatically. All customer orders were moved together to inventory management after having queued for a day; there a check was performed for all orders together to see if there was enough stock; next, they were again all moved together to be picked, and so on.

Materials requirement planning (MRP) systems were developed to help companies plan production and purchases better. But early MRP systems were only run on a weekly, sometimes monthly basis. As a consequence, many other activities within the company did not even have to be performed promptly. It was enough if customer orders, open purchase orders, and inventory levels were correctly recorded when the planning run was made.

This changed in the 1980s. Western companies suddenly realized that the functional approach would never yield the efficiency improvements needed to catch up with streamlined Japanese competitors. Michael Hammer[1] describes in his 1990 *Harvard Business Review* article: "Reengineering Work: Don't Automate, Obliterate," how Ford uncovered the need for process redesign. In the accounts payable function, Ford was aiming at cutting head count to 400 persons—a 20 percent efficiency improvement—until it discovered that Mazda was able to perform the same work with only 5 persons. This was a wake-up call to analyze the existing process across functions.

The result illustrates the weakness of a functional organization. Departments and units communicate by passing documents, either on paper or as file transfers between departmental computer systems. When ordering, the purchasing organization at Ford would send a copy of the purchase order to accounts payable. Similarly, at goods receipt, the materials control function would send a copy of the receiving document to accounts payable. The job of the accounts payable function was to match these two documents with the supplier invoice and pay the supplier. The problem was that frequently the three documents did not match. And, accounts payable spent almost all its time investigating discrepancies, creating work for the purchasing and materials control departments, as well as for the suppliers.

The solution was simple and illustrates how computers can create efficient processes across departmental boundaries. When the purchasing department issues an order, it is entered into an online database. This database is then also used at goods receipt by the materials control department. If a matching purchase order is found when the goods arrive, they are received and the supplier is paid by accounts payable. If there is no purchase order or the delivery does not match the order, the goods are returned to the supplier. No invoices are needed from the supplier, and the accounts payable department has no more discrepancies to investigate. As a result, the accounts payable department could be reduced by 75 percent, and unnecessary work with following up mismatches in other department could also be eliminated.

Inside a large organization, the key element for forging new efficient processes is sharing data between functions in real time, like the sharing of purchase order between the purchasing and materials control functions at Ford. The objective is to eliminate administrative tasks that were developed when information could only be shared by sending documents between functions. To create shared real-time processes within large companies, new IT technology was developed in the late 1980s to overcome the limitations of time and place. The result was Enterprise Resource Planning (ERP) systems.

Used correctly, ERP systems can have a big impact on cost efficiency, customer service, and inventory levels by tightly linking company functions. Ship-to-order can be speeded up using a predefined workflow that eliminates waiting and administrative delays between order administration, picking, and shipping. In assembly-to-order, making the availability check for materials and production capacity at order entry makes it possible for the supplier to give the customer an accurate delivery date. And, daily scheduling and purchasing to customer demand can drastically reduce the need for both finished goods inventory and material stocks, without undermining customer service.

This still leaves the limitation of different companies not sharing the same systems. Order, delivery, and billing documents need to be passed between companies and business units to initiate and complete transactions. Here, Electronic Data Interchange (EDI standards) and thin clients provide the technology to remove old barriers. A thin client is a solution where the logic run on a server, and on the user's computer there is only a program that interfaces the user to the server. Electronic documents make it possible to automate and speed up the interaction between trading partners. In the automotive industry in the 1980s, Western carmakers were struggling to catch up with the Japanese manufacturers and implement just-in-time supply. An EDI standard called Odette was created and adopted to speed up transactions between the carmakers and their major suppliers. In the grocery industry, new processes for a more efficient response to consumer demand and the adoption of enabling EDI technology speeded up the order to delivery process significantly. In the beginning of the 1990s, a response time of 48 hours was considered fast, but by the end of the decade, same-day delivery was the norm.

Electronic interchange of documents makes it possible to link supplier and customer IT systems, and speed up processing. However, the big innovation with EDI is not the electronic transfer as such, but the standardization of the message. The issue is that a supplier wants to use the same solution with as many customers as possible. In the same way, the customer wants to use the same solution with all suppliers. Setting up electronic links between companies was possible before EDI, but each time it was necessary to decide whether the supplier's existing solution or the customer's, or maybe a compromise, was to be used. To sum up, before EDI and the standardization of messages, the solutions between different companies were not scalable (not easily adopted with new trading partners).

Not that scaling up links between trading partners is easy with a standard, either. Before automating a link (e.g., the order), you still have to go through the process in fine detail to make sure that the supplier and customer systems understand the same piece of information, in the same way, in all situations (e.g., the unit for a specific product can sometimes be understood differently by the customer and the supplier). In this situation, the human ordertaker may have translated the consumer packages ordered by the customer into the wholesale cases used by the supplier before entering the order. But, before automating, the problem has to be resolved by having one of the parties change its definition.

But just as sharing an application between departments is a key enabler for business process reengineering inside a company, sharing applications between different business units and companies opens up opportunities for more radical change—new value offerings—by integrating with the customer's inventory management or business planning.

Already in the first half of the 1990s, thin clients—applications where the data and logic run on a server and the client is only an user interface as in SAP's R/3 system—made possible many of the things that World Wide Web applications do. That is, from anywhere in the world, an authorized user could access a business application. With a call-in modem, a salesperson could run a report or enter an order from a laptop computer. The limit was that users still needed a special program (graphical user interface), and also needed a user account and password for the application. Thus, with this technology, it was still difficult to reach new customers.

Supply chain planning and control systems use both standard data interchange and thin client technology. This is the foundation for coordinating units that previously were separate around a common objective—to improve service to end customer. After heavy restructuring in the mid 1990s, Unilever's detergents and household cleaning business in

Europe introduced a supply chain planning and control (SPC) system (Manugistics) to secure supply to smaller markets. But this required synchronization between sales companies and manufacturing—all sales companies, big ones included. As a result of the synchronization, inventory buffers between plant and trade customers were dramatically reduced.

Handling product variety is another area where new information technology has pushed back the limits of what can be handled operationally. Today it is possible to master product variety proactively, and thus increase the value without losing efficiency in production (i.e., we have mass-customized products). The enabling technology for mass-customized products is product configurators and product data management (PDM) systems. The basic solution is an application where the customer herself, or the supplier's salesperson, can specify product features and options before the product is built. Checking material availability and the capacity situation for the product gives the customer a reliable delivery date before placing the order. Where a salesperson does the configuration, a thin client solution is sufficient, but for sales to consumers, a Web solution is needed. (It is also necessary for first-time and occasional customers to have access to the configurator.)

Dealing with product variety by programming product features even makes it possible to configure products after purchase. For example, the consumer can change the honk of an automobile herself after she has purchased the car by going to the supplier's home page and downloading a new sound.

■ WHAT LIMITS ARE SET BY TECHNOLOGY TODAY?

Today's Web applications make it easier for companies to create new business by differentiating customer relationships and thus substantially increasing the value of relationships. In the past, vendor managed inventory, collaborative planning, and other advanced value offerings could be made only to a few key customers because of the high cost of setting up the solution with each new partner using EDI and value added networks. Now using Web-based applications, you can in a matter of minutes set up complex processes with new partners spanning many supplier and customer businesses.

The limits set by technology have been pushed much beyond what could have been imagined only 10 years ago. Today, technology makes it possible to:

➤ Eliminate order and invoice transactions altogether between grocery suppliers and retailers by the supplier replenishing and the retailer paying to scan at the point of sales.

➤ Reducing search costs for the customer to a fraction has reversed markets. Instead of suppliers seeking customers through marketing and sales activities, customers now increasingly seek out sellers online for products as diverse as building materials and vacations.

➤ Streamline functions and reduce fixed costs by outsourcing large sections of the demand-supply chain to information and logistics service providers.

➤ Achieve real-time integration and synchronization from the first day with a new supplier or customer by using Web applications that can be set up in minutes.

➤ Increase the value of products to a low cost through mass customization of programmable features over the Internet.

➤ Increase the value of the company's relationships to a point where both supplier and customer companies have made the relationship a separate business. By setting up a trading process network (info hub) and charging other companies for using the service, GE's purchasing organization spawned a totally new business with its TPN Register. Another example, from the sales side, is American Airlines with its SABRE registration system.

Looking ahead, the current range of innovative applications will converge into a small number of winning configurations. Just as internal processes based on information sharing were "canned" in standard ERP systems, various e-commerce applications will converge into only a few basic package types.

Online auctions, exchanges, vertical markets, and communities will change how companies organize their purchasing function. A new and efficient demand-supply chain configuration—an offer-to-purchase without a separate function to transact requirements—will emerge for commodities. Businesses have already started to integrate online purchasing, supplier and product data managed by reliable intermediaries, and purchasing aggregators directly with the internal business processes that drive demand. This will be a step toward a market where both the customer and supplier are able to act on accurate real-time information.

Shifting more responsibility for the business success of the customer to the supplier (i.e., moving the VOP) and integrating aftersales support into the delivery process drives developments toward the second winning package. Seller-centric Web sites, online help lines, and value added supply chain solutions such as in-plant stores, VMI, and collaborative plans create the foundation for vendor lock-in networks. In the United States, Heineken has developed a simple solution linking itself to the marketing and sourcing activities of over 400 beer distributors. A similar system—Philips Trade Link—to improve channel distribution and service is underway by Philips Lighting. The objective is to quickly scale up the solution from a pilot involving three key distributors to a comprehensive network integrating 400 distributors.

A third winning package is to integrate supply chain, knowledge management, and project management applications. These project hubs are the future foundation for efficiently coordinating complex relationships in the automotive and aerospace industries. After having developed their proprietary solution, Ford with its TradeXchange and GM with its AutoXchange decided to join forces to create a universal e-marketplace to manage engineering designs, orders, and inventory data with their suppliers. Immediately after the launch, other key players in the industry joined the venture.

Even more is possible. Cheap processors and wireless communication mean that products and components can get an identity and some processing capability. Instead of controlling the supply chain from above, and risk running into the complexity crisis of application spaghetti, we can develop simple solutions from the bottom up.

For example, each shipment could be programmed to maximize its profit. The manufacturer could just ship the product in the general direction with the best prices, or where demand exceeds supply. The task for the shipment would be to try to find the lowest cost way to the customer paying the best price by tapping into different online markets and markets for logistics services on the way. Thus, a new opportunity for a supplier in a competitive, but dynamic market would be to move the OPP from product in the warehouse to individual shipments already on the market. And in the process, the firm eliminates order administration, sales, and warehousing functions inside its own organization, and instead relies completely on the markets.

Also, by letting shipments and other devices communicate, new business models such as the "don't run out" service for groceries could be realized without advanced central control. This could be an important selling point to consumers worried about privacy—no big brother is checking your fridge—just a simple-minded milk carton that alerts a replacement when it is opened.

What will bring all this together? Forrester Research suggests that firms need to dismantle the traditional internal IT organization and disperse management across an external technology environment. The first sign of this trend is the use of ERP application hosting in successful new business models. For example, sharing IT solutions for buying and selling give even a small company the opportunity to quickly set up common business processes with new partners. Personalization and customization again can be leveraged for value innovation in the customer relationship.

With all this new "e" technology, there is a risk of losing sight of the actual business opportunities and getting nothing out. Always remember that the new innovating practices in demand-supply chain management are a result of a co-evolutionary process between technology and business application. Success is not guaranteed by the technology itself, but by its application.

■ THE BLEEDING EDGE—THE RISKS OF NEGLECTING YOUR DEMAND CHAIN FOR IT SOLUTIONS

In the early 1990s, client/server technology held the promise of making applications independent of organizational units and geographic locations. Attention centered on what could be achieved through computer integration in terms of productivity improvement and increased flexibility.

At that time, Gloco, a vertically integrated company with global operations, saw the opportunity to leapfrog competition in operational efficiency by developing a suite of client/server applications to link its production, distribution, and sales seamlessly. Gloco set out to develop a global ERP system in-house because no standard solutions were available. Ten years later, the application suite had been successfully developed, delivered to most business units in the supply chain, and become the operational backbone of the company's business. In the meantime, however, specialized solutions providers developed efficient standard solutions packages. Many competitors that moved to integrate operations later, now have in place solutions that capture value more effectively in a changing business environment.

There are several weak links in Gloco's IT strategy and execution. The IT solution and platform is an in-house development; it is only a standard solution for the company. The effect is that competitors using standard package alternatives support each other in the development of new business solutions, while Gloco has to bear all costs alone. Also, technology has moved away from Gloco's fat client solution to thin clients and browsers.

Competitors can more easily scale up their standard solutions over sites in merger situations and extend them to both suppliers and customers in a growing number of e-commerce initiatives. And, in the business use stage, the Gloco solution is more difficult to adapt to new situations. New business requirements frequently have to be accommodated in ad hoc pilot solutions or wait for the rollout of a new application module. In the competing companies, these opportunities are more readily captured through master data and process definitions in the business use stage.

So what is the point? Was Gloco too eager to apply new technology? No, it is not a matter of new technology, but how you manage the technology. Technology simply sets the limits; and if you are slow at capturing value, you will always be struggling to catch up. Gloco's problem was that it responded to IT opportunity the same way as to its business opportunities (by integrating vertically). The company did not consider appropriately the benefits from partnering with specialized solution providers, once it had a tested model ready for how it wanted to operate its business. Only too late, when competitors had already adopted a comparable standard solution, did the company realize that the envisioned competitive advantage from the investment would never materialize.

There is a difference between being a world-class user of information technology and a world-class provider that Gloco did not appreciate in time. For world-class users, it may make sense to use their own resources up to prototyping and piloting new approaches. But for developing scalable platforms that will need to be redeveloped regularly, you usually are better off partnering with a technology provider. (Or set up a new business to provide the technology to you and your competition.)

As business-to-business IT solutions become more common, specialized solution providers will be able to deliver better standard solutions. Eventually in this situation, further developments of an initially innovative application will yield only marginal improvements but require ever more resources. Then, having initiated development efforts in partnership with leading solution providers and sharing the application with competitors will prove valuable. The move will help the company solution become the industry standard and enable the innovator to better focus resources on new areas with bigger potentials. It was at this point that Gloco failed. Because it waited too long to partner with solution providers and to market its application to competitors, Gloco lost in the value capture game to less innovative, but more collaborative competitors.

Most companies are even less successful than Gloco. A Standish Group survey of 500 IT projects in the demand-supply chain domain indicates that more than half of all efforts fail, and two thirds of the remaining projects are only partly successful. The quoted reasons for failure were incomplete requirements, lack of user involvement, inadequate resources, unrealistic user expectations, lack of management support, changing requirements, and inadequate planning. Missing from the list of reasons for failure is technology, but despite this, companies still commonly focus on opportunities from applying new technology. In Chapter 9, we take an alternative viewpoint and focus on the opportunities from better management of IT applications.

REFERENCE

1. Michael Hammer, "Reengineering Work: Don't Automate, Obliterate," *Harvard Business Review,* July–August 1990, 104–112.

Chapter

Information Technology Value Capture—Linking IT Seamlessly to Business Opportunity

The IT value capture process both determines your starting point and whether you can ever reach your full potential.

■ INFORMATION TECHNOLOGY VALUE CAPTURE CHALLENGES

So, why is it important to focus on the use and delivery of IT applications, and not on technology alone? To answer this question, it is helpful to examine the link between new technology and its business use (value capture). A good starting point for thinking about the links is making the business case for IT technology in the demand-supply chain. The links that we look at are identifying the business opportunity of IT applications, managing the scale of IT solutions, designing the business solutions, and managing the resources for IT.

➤ Identifying Opportunity

Identifying business opportunity is no longer a separate marketing or business development process. Instead, it is part of both order fulfillment and IT systems development.

Because it is more efficient to sell more to the same customer than to acquire new customers, it makes sense to supply individual customers with a product range that is as wide as possible. For example, Amazon has expanded its supply side, moving from books to videos to healthcare products and later on to a large spectrum of consumer goods. But you can take action also on the customer's demand chain side. Würth moved with the same product range from the assembly, to maintenance, and on to the aftersales operations by creating new value added services for the customer.

To implement new value offerings systematically, and also with smaller customers, it is necessary to make self-service and service configuration an integral part of the customer relationship. The idea is to shift the focus from delivering a product or service to the customer, to providing the customer with the means to customize the relationship in the best possible way for himself or herself. Increasingly, the means for this are IT applications.

In many companies, Web-based sales applications are used to increase the value of the customer relationship by providing the customer with order proposals based on the customer profile. In this way, continuous relationship marketing—also known as database marketing, micromarketing, or one-to-one marketing—can bring marketing into the scope of order fulfillment.

➤ Managing Scale

The reduced limitation on the time and place where an IT solution can be used introduces a new element to IT value capture. This is managing where to use the solution, which can be tricky. Is it desirable to scale up a complex solution that tightly integrates organizations that formerly were separate, or is a simple solution that loosely links a large number of units and trading partners more desirable?

There are many examples of the difficulty to manage scale from ERP projects in multinational corporations. The key question is where should the same solution be used? What "backbone" is needed? It is often easy to see that high-level product data (product codes and product characteristics such as weight and size) should be the same everywhere in the supply chain. But it is much more difficult to decide whether sales and delivery routines should be standardized or are better left differentiated.

The difference is that a system for creating and maintaining product codes can be quickly and effectively adopted by a large number of production and sales units, whereas a standardized sales and delivery process cannot be. Simple differences in pricing and invoicing conventions and the use of different logistics partners on the local level can make it difficult to implement corporatewide sales and distribution solutions. (And in addition, it constrains the ability to capture local business opportunities.)

The minimum backbone requirement in a global company is dependent on the complexity of the collaborative business processes between units. If products, customers, and suppliers are all local for a business unit, no backbone is needed outside the domain of financial reporting. When the corporation has global sourcing ambitions, then the backbone at least has to cover common coding for purchased items and suppliers. If the ambition is global customer service, then the backbone function is common coding for customers and sales items. And, if the value offering is delivering a customized product or installation from business units around the world, then the backbone is project management.

The same basic logic can also be applied to collaboration between different companies. If the value offering is that a group of complementors complete turnkey projects globally, then the backbone is project management. If the collaboration is limited to buying and selling, then the minimum backbone is trade partner identification and product identification.

► Managing Solution Design

Standard technology solutions, such as integrated packages and standard data interchange messages, are major ingredients in many innovative demand-supply chains. These allow companies to create efficient new business processes by linking functions and trading partners without developing new applications themselves. Depending on the business solution design, the key tools can be either integrated solutions or standard messages, or both.

For example, parcel delivery companies like UPS and FedEx have developed integrated solutions for tracking. The customer uses the delivery company's application for tracking over the Internet, and with the help of the tracking number follows a shipment to its destination. On the other hand, an automotive factory that uses different logistics service providers may prefer that transportation companies send messages in a standard format from different points on the way. In the former case, the solution is to use a standard value added service provided by the supplier, and in the latter case a message that allows the customer to perform the tasks himself.

Today, the arguments for and against sharing applications or sending messages continue in the form of "best of breed" or standard solutions. A company that has enough clout to get other players to use its application is likely to argue in favor of standards and sharing services, while a company being pulled between many standards would be in favor of the best-of-breed approach and message standardization.

Technology providers are increasingly opting for more open and granular solutions, making it easier to combine diverse ERP systems on a business unit level with supply chain optimization tools on the chain level. This means that there will be an even wider range of different options open for designing a business.

The challenge for managing IT value in an abundance of alternatives is to keep a clear focus on the business configurations that improve both value offering and efficiency. The key principle again is self-service. Solution designs must be widely available for efficiency and possible to customize locally to enable value innovations. That is, the solution is modularity and Web access. The scale where the application is used is large (e.g., the corporation or supply chain), but the application is local, customized, or personalized.

➤ Managing Information Technology Resources

The goals of IT management are threefold:

1. Ensure IT brings value for costs.
2. Ensure IT is aligned with the business.
3. Ensure IT is positioned for the future.

These goals must be attained at the same time to ensure IT management creates value to the business. The evolution of IT technology has made managing IT to capture the opportunities more complex. Identifying new business opportunities as part of operations, managing the scale of solutions, and designing modular business solutions using standard messages and packages are activities that have become necessary as IT technology has evolved. However, the primary focus of IT management still is managing the resources needed to deliver and maintain IT services.

Despite the increased use of packages and application services, few companies capture value efficiently. In most companies, a closer look at how resources are used will reveal that they are scattered across low-value functions. Overhead, maintenance, systems engineering, operations, and help desk consume almost all available resources. Very little remains for developing new business applications and solutions for the customer (i.e., delivering the high value added functions made possible by technology).

The bottleneck is the lack of people skilled at systems selection, integration, networking, and middle ware solutions. As a consequence, many companies in industries with a rapid rate of change are opting to externalize technology and IT service supply.

■ THE INFORMATION TECHNOLOGY DEMAND-SUPPLY CHAIN—LINKING INFORMATION TECHNOLOGY SEAMLESSLY TO BUSINESS OPPORTUNITY

Then, how can you change the situation—shift the focus of IT to delivering high value added for the business?

In many businesses, "process owners" have the responsibility for delivering the value. The process owner is responsible for spotting process innovations early, driving continuous improvement and learning, as well as initiating the development and delivery of more efficient processes and IT tools.

Assigning responsibility is an important first step, but what does a process owner need to do to succeed in an environment increasingly shaped by IT? The key is to understand how to link the major IT functions into an IT supply chain; and, then, how to integrate this IT supply chain with the IT demand chain.

The IT supply chain takes technological opportunity and delivers solutions for running or supporting the business processes of the company. The IT supply chain consists of strategy and concept initiation, piloting and industrializing solutions, implementation, and business use.

The IT demand chain consists of identifying a business opportunity, determining the scope, innovating business solutions, and making the business case—the resource and partnering decisions.

The starting point for an IT development project is the business case or vision. In the business case needed to launch a big applications development project, you need to cover business opportunity, consider all the places and situations where the opportunity exists, outline the business design needed to capture the opportunity, and assess resource requirements to get it all done. But these are actually also the steps in the IT demand chain.

The IT demand chain gets rid of the "make the business case" task to launch individual IT projects, and replaces it with a continuous management process that links your business needs seamlessly to your solutions and technology providers.

Whereas the IT demand chain is the business case turned into a continuous feedback process, the IT supply chain is the IT project turned into a fulfillment process. In the IT supply chain, you initiate, pilot, industrialize, implement, and use technology to capture business value. Creating an IT demand chain is to set up a process that depending on the situation takes a business opportunity to the right stage in the IT supply chain, (i.e., initiate, pilot, industrialize, or implement).

When the IT demand-supply chain is well organized, most opportunities can be captured immediately, and only a few have to go to "initiate." A simple example is a salesperson using a sales statistic himself to make a new type of report, rather than requesting a new development from the IT department. The result is fast response and more business value.

In managing IT value, we really have two chains to consider: a demand chain and a supply chain (see Figure 9.1). There is a close analogy between the demand-supply chain for the business and the IT demand-supply chain for the business systems. In both cases, separating demand from

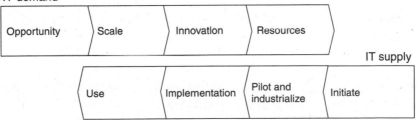

Figure 9.1   IT Demand-Supply Chain

supply makes it easier to redefine roles and find innovative new ways to improve responsiveness and efficiency in a changing business environment.

■ ESCAPING THE "BLEEDING EDGE," OR WHY START WITH DEMAND FOR INFORMATION TECHNOLOGY RATHER THAN TECHNOLOGICAL OPPORTUNITY?

Today, business and technology time lines are much shorter than the applications delivery lead time for new solutions. In the early 1980s, the typical product, technology, and applications development cycles were roughly in sync at five years. Since then, many industries have moved to a business cycle where new product generations are introduced every year, and many more to a pace of every two to three years. A business environment that changes much quicker accompanies the higher pace of product innovation. Companies need to set up new channels, enter new markets, and partner with different companies much more often and quickly than in the past.

At the same time, the rate is accelerating for new opportunities to apply IT technology in business. Processing and storage capabilities continue to double every few years, and bandwidth constraints for wire and wireless communication tumble for both consumers and businesses. However, medium-size and large applications development projects still require three to five years.

This is where the IT demand-supply chain becomes useful. You cannot capture value simply by developing new applications to respond to changing business needs: You cannot capture value if you always start over with developing concepts, building applications, rollout, and only then start using them. Going from end to end in the IT supply chain takes time, and the bigger the project the longer it takes.

You won't capture the business opportunities while they are still there with a develop-to-order approach (or at least you won't be the one to revolutionize the business model). What is needed is the ability to adapt to business change already in the use and implementation stages of the IT supply chain, and to simultaneously manage new technology through all the stages of the IT supply chain. This chain needs to be managed so that the architecture for both the current and future applications is scalable, flexible, and modular.

The IT demand-supply chain can be configured in several ways. Each new configuration contributes to increasing the total capability to capture business value from information technology. Figure 9.2 outlines the configurations.

The first configuration integrates business use with identifying new business opportunities. How do you identify requirements and ideas from users—the customers, business units, employees, and suppliers that use the application? The most effective way is obviously self-service. But you can also

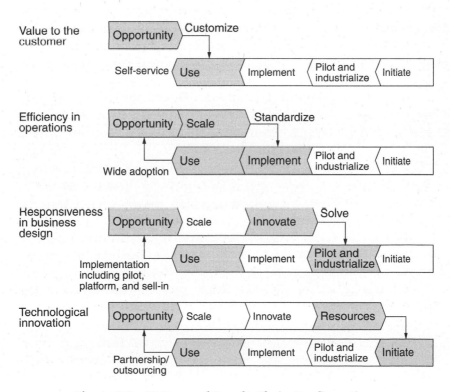

Figure 9.2   IT Demand-Supply Chain Configurations

encourage feedback and submission of suggestions online or in regular seminars and advanced user group meetings. The link back to the IT supply chain is customizing or personalizing the solution according to individual requirements.

The majority of opportunities can be captured immediately without moving upstream in the IT supply chain when the self-service offering and customization functionality are successful. But even when unsuccessful, it is important. In self-service applications, customization and personalization functions can be leveraged to collect new requirements. For example, if a user tried to define a new report for himself, but failed, collecting his feedback and description of what was wanted would be valuable input for later. The information could be used for defining enhancements when moving up the IT supply chain.

The second configuration gives a different perspective on: "How do you deliver enhancements?" The answer is not necessarily by new development, but by scaling up an existing standard solution. The objective is to use IT operations as much as possible for delivering enhancements. If the application platform is a standard solution package, it is sometimes possible to use solutions that have been developed as standard, but not yet been implemented by the company. Scaling up is IT operation's response to the IT demand chain's requirement for enhancements.

The third configuration is ideally needed much less than the previous two. Only if you do not see an obvious solution on your scalable and modular platforms (the business opportunity is completely new), is it necessary to move on to the next step in the IT demand chain. Based on new business design ideas, the objective is to develop and test pilot solutions, using, if possible, the existing modular platforms for the application. Formalizing the implementation approach and developing support tools to market the new business model are also important (i.e., industrialization).

The last configuration is needed to make technological innovation available in the business. The configuration links the IT demand chain with the supply chain through initiatives to create new technology and partnerships with technology providers.

Initiatives for new developments can be initiated through interest groups and industry partnerships. For example, the concepts and enabling technologies to support collaborative planning, forecasting, and replenishment are developed within a consortium of companies, the CPFR committee. The committee is one of six Voluntary Interindustry Commerce Standards (VICS) committees in the United States. Their mission is to create collaborative relationships between buyers and sellers through comanaged processes and shared information. The participating companies are looking for opportunities to apply the results in their business operations, and provider companies are looking for new product and service ideas.

The four preceding configurations are not alternatives, but complement each other.

It is essential to allot enough resources to support the development of new IT concepts and strategies, as they provide the foundation for alternatives that can replace the applications and platforms currently in use.

It also is critical to understand that collaboration in the IT demand-supply chain often pays off better than keeping to yourself. Few companies today can create really new approaches and technologies on their own. It is not the company that first spots an opportunity to innovate, but the one with an innovative solution in wide use that gets the competitive advantage. Companies like Wal-Mart, Procter & Gamble, and Hewlett-Packard are mobilizing industrywide support for new development initiatives within the CPFR committee, confident in their ability to gain competitive advantage through value capture rather than IT development.

■ IDENTIFYING OPPORTUNITY IN BUSINESS USE— STRETCHING THE LIMITS FOR CUSTOMER VALUE

The stage closest to the business in the IT supply chain is business use. This is also the place to start a detailed analysis, because any weakness in the IT demand-supply chain as a whole surfaces at the latest here.

The key objective of managing the IT demand-supply chain is stretching solutions to their maximum potential.

This requires resources—application specialists and super users—as well as solutions that support individual requirements. The ideal is that even in new situations it should be possible for the individual user, whether an employee, a customer, or a supplier, to get the needed work done without disruption or delay. The role of the help desk is to resolve those issues that the user herself cannot deal with.

Business use and help desks become more important when applications cross organizational units, and reach suppliers, customers, and consumers. The sheer number of users in e-sales and purchasing solutions makes it critical that self-service works intuitively and is responsive to new needs discovered by users as they gain experience. It is here, in the user interaction with the application that the IT demand-supply chain is stretched to the limits.

Using a self-service application, the user should be able to make step-by-step better use of an IT solution. Dell can set up a basic Premier Page for a new customer in a few minutes. After this, the customer has a solution to manage PC purchases according to a corporate standard that she can define without further involvement of Dell's IT operations. For example, the customer can start to export data from Dell's systems and manually enter product specifications to their asset management system. And then, give the help desk for its own enterprise resource planning (ERP) the task to create automatic imports needed to streamline payments, general ledger, and omit management tasks.

A help desk close to business users increases the value of a system significantly; it makes responses to new situations faster. In ERP systems, a business user who needs to check delivery precision to a customer using the customer's definition of performance may find that the standard reports and statistics are not adequate. In this situation, many companies that have just started using a new system respond to all reporting needs in the same way. It is a task for applications development (i.e., the pilot and industrialization stage) of the IT supply chain. The business user has to make a request, which is prioritized, next an analyst makes a specification, and finally a programmer makes the new report. This cumbersome process may require several days of work, and the result is often a report with many errors. By responding to the needs of business users through a help desk, the same information can be retrieved in an hour using a report writer or query, with no programming errors. (Or, even better, the help desk can point the user to an existing report.)

How do you know what to deal with on a user level, and what on operations or a development level? The principle is that adjusting available solutions to new situations is the realm of business use and the help desk. For example, collaborating with suppliers and customers on master data can reduce the complexity of solutions radically. So, if a standard product catalog or collaboration process to share product data (e.g., UCCnet) already is available, then simply try to use it for a new product attribute (e.g., product category) that needs to be synchronized. If there are problems that cannot be resolved, then it becomes a development issue. And, if the other party does not have access to the same solution as you do, it may be an issue for your IT operations.

How you manage business use and help desk can also increase the responsiveness to new requirements. For self-service applications, feedback and new requirements to drive value capture can be collected through user groups and conferences. A direct benefit from having different users meet and discuss experiences and needs is expanding the scope of a solution used in one situation to other users. The feedback process is crucial to identify new business opportunities, such as to start a pilot to probe potential new solutions, explore innovative ways of doing business, identify the need to create new technology, and consider prospective new technology and service providers.

■ IMPLEMENTATION—DELIVERING THE SOLUTIONS AND RESULTS EFFICIENTLY

If the front-line configuration of the IT demand-supply chain is the key to capturing new business opportunities, the demand-supply configuration one step upstream is critical for efficiency.

The objective of implementation is delivering the best available solution to each business situation. It is through the demand-supply configuration at this stage that the company realizes the competitive potential of its concept and application development efforts.

The effect of an innovative solution that is used in just one business unit or with a handful of local customers is low. Also, the business potential is not fully accomplished when the rate of adoption of the new solution is slow. In many companies, this is a serious obstacle for value innovation.

In many supplier companies, vendor managed inventory has been abandoned because the cost of managing customer inventory exceeds the supplier benefit in inventory reductions. To see results on the company level, a big share of volume needs to be to VMI customers. For a supplier, the effects of replacing inventory with better information are not significant until VMI customers represent a fifth of total sales. The time to reach this level depends partly on the channel structure, but above all on how effectively the supplier can extend the solution to new customers.

The importance of scaling up innovations, not just innovating is emphasized because of the Internet. Heineken's U.S. operations is a case in point. In 1995, Heineken had just bought back the distribution rights for the United States from a private company. Heineken was faced with a backward sales and marketing organization that focused solely on pushing goods to distributors. There were no IT solutions at all to support sales and distribution, and no active sales force working with the distributors to create demand pull.

To meet Heineken's aggressive business development goals for the U.S. market, a solution that would make it possible to work as a small supplier with a network of 450 distributors was quickly needed. Most of the distributors had already integrated solutions with large domestic breweries such as Miller or Coors. In this situation, Heineken needed a simple solution that distributors could adopt with minimum effort. The solution was to create an Internet-based platform—HOPS—to quickly reach its distributors with a new offer to planning value proposition.

With the new value offering, distributors simply need to report once a month their sales, current inventory, and sales forecast. Orders were completely eliminated: Heineken replenishes according to sales plan from its breweries in Holland. Inventory levels are adjusted with the same monthly cycle according to how distributor sales turned out.

With typically less than 10 percent of a distributor's volume, Heineken could place limited hopes on its customers' development resources in the operations stage of the IT supply chain. Because of this, the application for the new value offering had to be very easy to extend to new distributors. The creation of a new distributor in the system is a matter of minutes. The setup of the collaborative process and user training, again, can be handled in a day. In the first pilot market, the advantages over competitor setups were already evident. The Florida distributor that became the first customer to adopt the new collaborative business process had only shortly before completed a conventional EDI-based project with a large domestic brewery. Whereas the Heineken solution was up and running in a day, the solution with the domestic brewery had taken weeks to complete.

The biggest obstacle to scaling up the new value offering was that distributors were leery of Heineken taking control. To overcome the obstacle, sell-in had to be improved, particularly demonstrating the benefits to smaller distributors.

Three years after the first pilot, the new collaborative business model was implemented with close to all of Heineken's 450 distributors. Previously stalled sales have increased 25 percent due to the new focus on consumer demand, rather than sales to the trade. Two thirds of distributors rate Heineken's new order placement and fulfillment as very good, compared with only one third in 1995. The revamped forecasting and planning have improved freshness and reduced inventory in the pipeline at the same time as the product range has been extended from 26 stock-keeping units to 42.

At Hewlett-Packard, when different business units started to adopt collaborative business processes, they realized that they could use the same IT and sell-in solutions even though there were big differences in the business models of the units. The collaborative solutions that were initially piloted by the unit selling HP's hard copy product line have been expanded step-by-step to include the product lines of other HP units in an ongoing offer-to-inventory management initiative to 30 retail distributors. The approach is to first sell-in the new value offering to a group of distributors, and then scale up step-by-step by adding more product lines. (Building from this basis, the distributors can expand the collaboration to more suppliers, which prepares the ground for making the offer-to-inventory management a de facto standard.)

Today, with good suppliers, purchasing is redundant and can be replaced by supplier management. Also, the same collaborative approach can be used for the IT supply chain. It is not necessary to wait for business units to discover the need for a new solution, or to force solutions on the organization in a rollout. The alternative is to fashion IT operations with a strong sales and marketing component both for external and internal solutions.

IT operations is not a support function responsible for systems rollout and maintenance, but a sales and marketing function for delivering and maintaining effective business solutions to business units, customers, and suppliers. This requires a business-minded IT operations and an organizational framework with analysts in both IT and in the business.

Resolute top management actions are sometimes needed to get a results-oriented IT operation off the ground. Eliminating sales commissions may be necessary to level the playing field and integrate IT operations with sales and marketing.

■ PILOTING AND INDUSTRIALIZATION—BUILDING THE SOLUTIONS AND PLATFORMS FOR RESPONSIVE BUSINESS REDESIGN

The next stage in the IT supply chain is piloting and industrialization. Opportunities that business users cannot immediately capture or scale up from other units or service providers need to be developed and tested. If the IT demand-supply chain is configured right, piloting and industrialization will focus on solutions to support new value innovations.

➤ Basic Building Blocks

The application selection and development is a key step in the IT supply chain. Because IT applications can be integrated, layered, distributed, modularized, and customized in many ways, it is appropriate to first look at the basic building blocks of an application. From the perspective of a value capture in the business use and operations stages these blocks are master data, transactions, procedures or methods, messages, and processes:

➤ Master data in IT applications defines the different entities involved in the business. Customers, products, suppliers, employees, warehouses, order types and terms of payment are all described using master data. The purpose of master data is to effectively organize information that is needed often (e.g., the delivery addresses of customers, and occasional changes to those addresses).

➤ A transaction is an action that produces a result. For example, order entry is the transaction that produces an order, and a query is a transaction to produce a report.

➤ Procedures or methods are used in transactions to get the desired result. For example, pricing is the method used to make sure that the customer order has the right price.

➤ Messages are a practical way to link transactions. For example, an order message can be used to link the purchase transaction of your customer with your order entry transaction.

➤ Processes, or work flows, in IT applications link all the transactions needed to produce a business result.

> To get the right product to the right customer, an application may have an order-to-delivery process linking order entry, shipping, and invoicing.

Technology providers often talk in terms of modules and functionality, but it is more practical to think of a module as an application that performs a set of processes and transactions. Because the trend is toward more open solutions, it is important to avoid confusing individual IT applications with the business solution.

The basic building blocks of an application affect the downstream IT supply chain in many ways.

Master data is the key to modular and adjustable applications. An application that defines how the customer is served using master data makes it possible to adjust the customer service processes on the fly in the business use stage. Using master data to define processes and standard messages also makes changing scope easier (faster setup for extending the process to new partners). Faster and easier setup means that you can extend the scope of innovative value offerings to smaller customers, even consumers.

How processes are setup can also have profound effects. Ideally, transactions are just fired off one after the other, and exceptions are dealt with using a new transaction. Often, however, there is a temptation to complicate things—just in case. For example, in an ERP system you can configure the picking transaction so that the warehouse is required to report back item by item to the order office. This seems a rather innocent arrangement for making sure there are no errors. But, as a matter of fact, this interactive picking process between warehouse and order office can be a real obstacle later in the IT supply chain. If the company decides to outsource shipping and warehousing, it is an unnecessary hassle to return to the development stage and find a solution for the new warehouse—with a new system—to report back line by line.

Instead, it is much more efficient to have a solution from the beginning that lets the warehouse know what needs to be picked and shipped using a standard message. With this solution, it is necessary for the warehouse to report back if and only if, the product happens to run out when the inventory management system indicated there should still be stock left (i.e., errors are highly unlikely). And, for the company, the message solution makes it possible to change warehouses without changing its order-to-delivery process in the IT system.

When setting up processes, it is useful to remember that interactive, human involvement is critical for supporting identification of new opportunities in the business use stage. Order picking, however, is an unlikely candidate for identifying business opportunity. Interaction is much more valuable in the form of a monthly collaborative planning process to support automated replenishment.

Simple procedures and methods, controlled through master data, are other areas where application development can make an impact downstream in the IT chain. It makes it easier to automate routine tasks and reduce friction with trading partners.

The basic application building blocks not only have implications for the downstream IT supply chain, but also upstream. Especially regarding master data and messages, there is a feedback loop. For example, using product and customer master data administered by a third party makes it easier to scale up solutions for customers and suppliers.

This point links to the initiate stage. In practice, a group for IT technology and collaboration is needed to identify standards and service providers for master data definitions and message standards.

➤ Solution Development

The key activity in the pilot and industrialization stage of the IT supply chain is development, the actual implementation of a solution that works and can be made available where needed. From a value capture perspective, it is advantageous to find a solution without initiating new concept and IT strategy development.

For example, a packaged consumer goods supplier was discussing a new offering with a key customer. The basic supply chain development actions—simplified pricing and continuous replenishment based on daily EDI purchase orders—had been implemented with good results. Encouraged by the results, both the supplier and customer were eager to pursue further improvements, and vendor managed inventory (VMI) had been identified as the next step. However, neither party had any experience setting up an offer-to-inventory management relationship.

Instead of rushing forward and starting to shop for ready solutions, the companies decided to set up a simple trial. The concept—replacing customer purchasing with vendor replenishment—seemed straightforward enough, but what new processes, master data, and messages were needed? The quickest way to find out would be to just do it with a few selected products.

In the trial, the development manager from the supplier company acted as a buyer in the customer company for half a dozen products. The development manager made the replenishment orders directly in the customer's purchasing system, based on the reorder point and a stock report with the free stock in the customer's distribution center. The next step was sending the inventory report by e-mail, and setting up a spreadsheet application on the supplier side. To make the replenishment order, the only additional information needed was the reorder point and delivery batch parameters for each item. Fast goods receipt became necessary when increasing the replenishment frequency to once every day. Whenever the customer had not received the replenishment order before the next inventory report was sent, the supplier replenished again. The solution for speeding up goods receipt was to send advance notice of the replenishment delivery to the customer's system.

At the supplier, new master data and a new transaction to create a replenishment order were necessary. In addition, for a daily replenishment process to work, an advance shipping notice from the supplier was essential to speed up goods receipt by the customer.

Getting the right building blocks for a solution only takes care of half the job. To be valuable for the business, both from a customer and vendor point of view, it must be possible to extend the VMI solution to new partners. What is needed is not only a pilot, but also a platform. It would appear that VMI is a good target for outsourcing—that the third party could act as the platform.

However, the solutions available from value added network operators at the time were both complex and expensive, in relation to the simple pilot. From the customer perspective, a third party would add no value, since the same messages and transactions were needed regardless of a third party or suppliercentric design. For the supplier, the only tricky issue with the solution was managing customer-specific inventory, and inventory control parameters.

Having focused the design on a handful of critical issues, the next task, finding a solution that could be used with a large number of partners was easy. The platform existed already on the supplier side. "Consignment," (setting up customer-specific inventory) was possible in the supplier's ERP. A customer-specific material master also existed for defining the control parameters. This was all that was needed to set up a transaction that replenished based on the customer's inventory level, and that could be extended to new customers simply by master data setup.

What has the application selection and development stage to offer the IT value capture process? First, by piloting alternative concepts the application stage offers tested solutions. Second, by arriving at the solutions through trials and pilots—thus eliminating just-in-case requirements—the application stage can produce simple platforms that can be effectively rolled out.

A good application platform includes not just the solution, but also support for selling-in the solution and scaling up. When different organizations are involved, rolling out is really selling-in. And, especially when dealing with customers, the implementation must not be a long and complicated process. The ideal is that a new customer can be reached with the application simply by registering, and configuring a restricted number of standard features to the requirements of the customer. The goal is to show a big potential benefit with a limited effort from the customer side.

To sell-in an application to a customer, the question you need to answer is, Why is it worth the attention and effort? Selling-in a solution is also a form of training and agreeing on common goals and objectives. This means that the sales-support part of a solution often is a combination of analysis and reporting. For example, the time profit analysis is an effective tool to support a VMI solution. Time profit shows the benefit of moving the VOP to inventory management in the first place—to support the operations stage of the IT supply chain. But it also can be used in the business use stage as a key performance indicator to alert when the situation changes and the benefit from an offer to inventory management disappears.

The implementation approach—scale-up—is also part of the platform and needs development effort. Formalizing a successful incremental development process can be an effective approach. In supply chain planning and control, results show that the median time to reach the different supply chain members is reduced by 50 percent with a results-driven incremental approach. Robert Fichman, of Boston College, and Scott Moses, of i2, describe in the *Sloan Management Review* how companies discover trouble more quickly if they follow an implementation approach that focuses on results through rapid increments, implementation segments, and throwaway work-arounds.[1] Implementing this way, companies are able to adjust better and rapidly realize more benefits.

A results-driven incremental approach links selling-in with implementation and following up with new developments to capture the full benefits. How can a supplier prepare through better applications development for the successful implementation of a new demand-supply chain configuration? For an offer to inventory management, we need to think of three issues. The first issue is to support selling-in and defining the goal for each customer implementation. Here, developing a tool for time profit analysis supports goal-setting: the same level of customer service for all products regardless of volume. Only now, we come to the actual application. To reach a large number of customers, we need a platform, a solution that is easy to set up. An

ERP-based vendor managed inventory solution that can be implemented with new customers using a standard message and master data fits that bill. And finally, how can the full benefits to the supplier be realized? For example, does a more level demand enable a consolidation of warehouses? In that case, a solution for sharing warehouses between sales organizations may need to be prototyped even before the first customers have accepted the new VOP.

■ INITIATION—FINDING ALTERNATIVES, NOT SETTING REQUIREMENTS, FOR TECHNOLOGICAL INNOVATION

The final stage in the IT supply chain that you need to reach through the IT demand chain is initiating technology and partnership initiatives.

Once an opportunity to improve the business with IT technology is perceived, many companies immediately shift focus from business to technology. In doing this, they entirely skip the first and most critical step in the IT supply chain, which deals with creating alternative concepts and IT strategy.

Critical business issues need to be identified because only by being crystal clear on the issues can you identify alternative solutions and their constraints. The key to creating new value from IT technology is finding alternatives, not setting requirements!

One framework to ensure the alternatives approach above the requirements approach is to ask the business side (e.g., the process owner) to define business imperatives at a level that allows one to select alternatives. Only then does he proceed to define the implications in terms of key processes and transactions jointly with IT and assess the alternatives. Well managed, the interaction between process owner and IT supply chain eliminates the need for a tedious and exhaustive requirements process.

The following list of critical business issues for an original equipment manufacturer illustrates the appropriate level of detail for order fulfillment:

➤ How does your customer know what you have to offer, and where?

➤ How do you know what your customer wants to buy, and when?

➤ How and when do you get paid?

➤ How do your suppliers and production know what parts to build and when?

➤ How and when do you pay your suppliers?

➤ How can you prevent competition weakening your relationship to your most profitable customers, and best suppliers?

Identifying the critical business issues up front makes it possible to find a limited number of simple and effective alternative concepts, as opposed to long lists of system requirements. The benefit is that alternatives are easier to communicate and understand than requirements lists. And, seeking alternatives prepares you for capturing new opportunities as they present themselves, instead of bogging you down in detailed issues.

For example, ERP software packages are built to deal with a wide range of industries and business needs. A company that has not identified the critical business issues runs the risk of choosing just-in-case solutions. A typical just-in-case solution is to frequently run materials requirements planning (MRP) to generate planned production and purchase orders. However, the critical issue for suppliers and manufacturing is knowing which parts are needed and when. Basic and stable parts are always needed, and a simple alternative to frequent MRP runs is to build to rate, to replenish. Many other parts (e.g., options) are also continuously needed, but the exact quantities vary. Here, an alternative could be to use the "3C" approach (see Chapter 5) to manage the flow of parts efficiently and without frequent replanning, or to set the planning strategy according to the demand.

Another example is asking functional departments to define requirements for collaborative customer solutions. Here logistics will immediately list requirements to optimize truck loads, sales will express concerns on executing campaigns to meeting sales targets, and finance will not allow any changes that postpone payment of goods delivered. When considering all the requirements from different departments, only a complex best-of-breed solution may appear possible. But the real issue is getting more reliable information on demand from more customers, and using this to add more value. Looking at the issue from this perspective, a robust VMI solution that can be easily implemented, based for example on ERP functionality, with a large number of customers is an alternative worth taking account of. Similarly, the pay-by-scan technology is not to be looked down on simply for reasons of postponed customer payments, because at the same time, it is an opportunity to gain daily access to point of sales data.

Thus, alternative concepts need to be developed to address critical business issues in the first stage of the IT supply chain. But alternative concepts are needed not only to support applications selection and development but also to identify alternatives for operations and business use. Self-service for customers and suppliers in the business use stage can be a powerful alternative to integrating systems. And for operations, partnering with a technology provider may enable you to scale up quicker to lower cost by spinning off cutting-edge solutions. Typical approaches are a joint venture/equity based approach, a technology consortium, and pure joint development efforts.

The value net is a tool to assess your value added in relation not only to your customers, but also to suppliers, competitors, and complementors (see Chapter 2). This bird's-eye view is necessary when deciding what to do yourself and where to use partners (i.e., in formulating IT strategy). The basic strategic choice is where in your value net you prefer to locate IT solutions and services.

Until recently, point-to-point solutions were the norm for demand-supply chain solutions. In this setup, the supplier and customer share the solution, that is, both have a degree of control. Typically, a combination of ad hoc file transfers and standard EDI messages are used for communicating, but this really is not the problem. You get problems even if you use the Internet. The complication arises when both the supplier and customer redesign (modify) their own systems solutions to accommodate each partner. As a consequence, when the number of partners grows, it becomes increasingly cumbersome to add new partners and modify established setups. Eventually, everything is connected to everything, and development grinds to a halt. We have a complexity crisis—or a "spaghetti" system shared by many different companies—on our hands.

Another option is for one party to take the lead—move into the complementor role in the value net—and go for a buyercentric or sellercentric design. In a buyercentric design, the customer supports the collaborative process, and the supplier simply provides inputs. In a sellercentric design, it is just the opposite. The supplier defines the process, and the buyer serves himself (does the work). The benefit with one or the other party taking the lead is that now there is a standard that can be developed and maintained much more efficiently. Dell's Premier pages is a sellercentric solution where customers can help themselves to new services as they are developed by Dell. UPS and FedEx are other examples of sellercentric designs where customers can help themselves to new functionality (e.g., interfaces to purchasing systems).

The trade-off for a company is to decide whether it wants to carry the fixed costs associated with providing the solution, but be in control, or be content with doing the work required by the other party to get the benefits. A company that has opted for control is Hewlett-Packard. The company is creating a hub to serve as the platform for collaboration both with its customers and its suppliers. That is, Hewlett-Packard has decided to be in control of the demand chains from its customers and sales channels, as well as its own demand chains to components suppliers.

If both parties in a relationship have the same strategy, either to minimize fixed costs or stay in control of the process, there is a problem. This is where a third-party solution provider—a dedicated complementor—comes into the picture.

With a third party providing the solution, your competitor can usually use the same solution. But more importantly, you can use the solution more easily with customers or suppliers. Network externalities come into play here. When a third party becomes a hub in the demand chain, competitors for customer demand are complementors in the efforts to extend the scope of more efficient demand-supply chain configurations. The efficiency benefits of an information hub in the demand chain are not very different from those of cross-docking and other collaborative solutions on the supply side.

But it is not necessary to use an intermediary to collaborate efficiently with suppliers and customers. Distributed solutions are also an option. The Internet itself best illustrates what is required to achieve a distributed solution strategy. There must be clear rules for joining, and a simple protocol for participating that is not dependent on any individual participant. Then an intermediary is not needed, just someone responsible for administrating the key master data—the identifiers of the participants.

UCCnet is a recent example. UCCnet is a distributed trading community that is supported and sponsored primarily by the U.S. grocery industry. The basic function of the net is to support trading partners in handling product master data collaboratively: how product items are organized, accessed, and exchanged between two parties, but not how the information is actually used. The objective is to create a common mechanism to share product data, which is used by both technology providers when developing new applications and by buyers and sellers when developing new demand-supply chains.

The choices made have an impact on the business use and help desk stage. A sellercentric approach gives the supplier better opportunities to efficiently customize solutions for customers. But the customer cannot use the same solution with other suppliers. There are also consequences for IT operations. Scaling up is easier if you cooperate with competitors and other suppliers of your customers. But control of the application is important in successfully setting up low-risk probes and piloting value innovations. Dependence on a third party can be a serious obstacle for piloting new innovative operations.

The initiation stage of the IT supply chain must offer the following to the value capture process:

➤ Positioning for the future by ensuring that the business can take advantage of emerging technologies.

➤ Maximizing leverage out of IT spend-through partnerships and outsourcing.

These goals can be met through focusing on business implications of IT by developing alternative concepts instead of detailed requirements, and balancing complexity against flexibility in outsourcing and collaboration decisions.

■ CONCLUSION—TECHNOLOGY SETS THE LIMITS, BUT MANAGEMENT GETS THE RESULTS

We have now examined the IT demand-supply chain and its impact on the business. The objective is to capture business benefits today, while avoiding large-scale IT technology renewal tomorrow. This means that the business needs to take advantage of emerging technologies and that the IT technology and architecture in use must coevolve—be continuously aligned—with the business opportunities.

The key points are:

➤ Technology sets the limits, management creates the value. Success is not guaranteed by new IT technology itself but by the application of the technology.

➤ To reach full potential, a continuous management process is needed to link the identification of business opportunity seamlessly to solutions and technology providers.

How do you link identifying your business opportunities seamlessly to your solutions and technology providers? The answer is to apply a demand-supply chain approach to IT.

From a demand perspective, the business captures value by identifying opportunity, setting the scope, looking for innovative solutions through detailing the business implications (the devil is in the details), and identifying the necessary business resources and solution providers.

From a supply perspective, IT needs to deliver value by having a clear IT vision and strategy (focusing on opening up

---

DELL'S PREMIER PAGES

Dell's Premier Pages for corporate customers illustrates an effective IT demand-supply chain. The corporate customers can themselves customize the use, and through this approach, Dell immediately captures many new business opportunities. Local sales and marketing organizations also function as a help desk for the business customers, introducing new services for individual customers. For customer requirements that cannot be resolved by the local sales and marketing organization, there is a central support organization. In Europe, Dell's sales and marketing are supported by a development center in the United Kingdom. New concepts are evaluated here, and frequently a solution already exists that can be introduced to the customer situation. When it is truly a new opportunity, business concepts are evaluated, piloted, and delivered through the Premier Pages platform in 3 to 6 months.

The Premier Pages platform is also evolving. It was initially launched in 1996, but by 1998 it was getting too complex to develop further. However, a new version—the Premier Pages II—had already been developed. In essence, Dell initiated the development of a new version in parallel with the one in business use. When it was no longer possible to improve the old platform, the new one was taken into operation. In the initiative stage of the IT supply chain, the company is also developing alternatives to the self-service approach. In Germany and the United Kingdom, pilots with direct integration to corporate customers' ERP-supported purchasing processes have already been completed. Trials are also underway with eliminating purchasing altogether by integrating with the hiring process of the corporate customers.

new alternatives for the business), making the appropriate architectural and software choices available, and securing the staffing and competence for effective implementation and profitable business application.

A company that cannot reduce the proportion of new opportunities that require a response in application development will not be able to reach its full potential. The trick is to stop thinking in terms of business case for individual IT projects and replace it with a continuous management process that links identifying your business opportunities seamlessly to your solutions and technology providers.

REFERENCE

1. Robert G. Fichman and Scott A. Moses, "An Incremental Process for Software Implementation," *Sloan Management Review,* Winter 1999, 39–52.

Chapter

Wireless Communication Revolutionizes the Demand-Supply Chain

While electronic commerce has opened up new opportunities for value innovations in the demand-supply chain, wireless communication, and especially wireless Internet, has the potential to revolutionize it. Mobility is the missing piece for finally creating demand-supply chains driven directly by end user demand, not by orders and forecasts.

The ubiquity of Internet makes it possible to reach all businesses and many consumers, but the ubiquity of mobile communication makes it possible to reach anyone and anything (e.g., cars, vending machines, containers, and tractors), anywhere, anytime. What does this mean for the demand-supply chain? The issue is:

What are the potentials for value innovations based on a person's and/or product's identity and location?

The answer is that there are significant value innovation opportunities in both the business-to-consumer and the business-to-business domain: The potential for revolutionizing the demand-supply chain through wireless communication is gigantic.

■ TRADING PROCESS—LINKING DEMAND AND SUPPLY

Before assessing the potential of wireless communication, let's consider the impact the Internet and wireless communication have already had in linking demand and supply.

With the ubiquity of the Internet, buyer companies can go out and ask for customized service from a large number of supplier companies. The basis for this is a standardized trading process, and the collaboration between many large buyers. Examples are the trading process collaboration between GE and other large U.S. original equipment manufacturers, and the automotive exchange set up by the big carmakers, with GM, Ford, and Daimler-Chrysler in the lead.

The key to make it all work is the request for proposal (RFP), and the screening of suppliers. The buyer's critical concerns are to reach a large number of qualified suppliers and to have these suppliers make relevant and competitive offers for serving the buyer. For the supplier, the critical concern is that it can quickly and effectively zoom in on its best available opportunities. The objective is also to help suppliers make creative (value added) offers to fulfill customer-specific demands. If it all works, the buyer gets a better customized service and the supplier can leverage its strengths optimally.

The next wave is mobile commerce. This makes it possible to set up trading processes where the requests and offers are contingent on location, and not only on a request for proposal. But at the moment, people and products on the move are still chained to the wired Internet, and the necessity to actively make the connection by call-in modem or barcode scanning. The key to make it all work again is a standard way to request service and a qualified screening of suppliers—to open up the demand chain for potential partners' value innovations. Even though existing applications mostly focus on business-to-consumer opportunities, there are huge potentials in the business-to-business domain.

Mobility in business benefit terms means that customers, partners, and employees can be supported and served by the information resources of a supplier wherever and whenever they allow it. When the customers make their demand chains visible in real time, the supplier can proactively or interactively optimize its offering in both time and place. The different stages of mobility can be divided into four major steps from the customer's point of view:

1. *Traditional wired.* Customer seeks the service.
2. *Wireless.* Customer seeks personalized service while on the move.
3. *Localized wireless.* The exact location of the customer can be one of the personalized service parameters, and service can even seek the customer itself.
4. *Authenticated wireless.* Authentication of the customer makes reliable payments and transactions possible, and personalized service can even recognize the customer while on the move.

These mobility development steps can be realized within and across different kinds of networks: Internet, extranet, corporate networks, and so on. The implication is that we can build up the new value offerings in both closed and open environments. Another key enabling development is the improvement in media richness (bandwidth): We are moving from text to wireless imaging to interactive mobile multimedia, which will significantly improve the richness of the data and services we can deliver.

Each of these development steps will have major implications for different business models and will create new value innovation opportunities in the areas of service differentiation and personalization, customer intimacy, speed, responsiveness, operational efficiency, and security.

In the consumer-to-business area, mobile commerce applications give supplier businesses the opportunity to customize offers, as consumers go about their daily business. The first piece of the puzzle is a consumer profile that serves as a "request for proposals" and screens out suppliers. The second piece is a way for the supplier to know the location of the consumer, and the third component is electronic payment.

To demonstrate how opening up the demand chain via wireless (making the request for customized offers based on a profile and location) works in an authenticated wireless environment, consider the following example.

A businessperson arriving for the first time in Helsinki has set up a personal profile indicating the type of rental car, hotel, entertainment, and restaurants that she enjoys. When she switches on her mobile phone in the airport, the profile is made visible to potential suppliers of hospitality and travel services. The profile screens out offers from all suppliers that are not certified by the airline's loyalty program and the credit card company.

While collecting her baggage, she receives an offer as a short message on her phone for the exact car she likes to drive and accepts the offer by replying to the message. When she leaves the airport, she sees that the car is already parked outside. She knows the car is for her as the car unlocks its doors when she approaches. On the way to Helsinki, she receives several offers for accommodation and decides to take a look at a particular hotel. The driving directions are conveniently displayed on the dashboard, and driving up to the hotel situated on the waterfront in a residential area, she decides to take the room. She accepts the offer by sending the hotel a standard short message with the duration of the stay and the billing information from her mobile phone. Walking through the lobby, she is automatically recognized and checked in. The receptionist greets her by name, as she can see on the computer screen details of the customer's profile made available while she is staying there. The receptionist notes that she likes jogging and gives her a map of the local jogging trails.

Mobility in the trading process means that the combination of request for proposals and the location of the customer trigger the supplier offers and responses. The basic mobile-commerce applications to make it possible are the customer profile and the localization. However, mobile payment, security, advertising, and telematics are also critical for a frictionless trading process between the mobile consumer and supplying businesses.

The mobile business-to-business applications developed at the moment are not yet as innovative as the preceding business-to-consumer scenario. Employees can get mobile access to supply chain IT systems, for example, to make an availability check, reserve goods, or order. Sales force automation, and management of fleets of distribution trucks are also applications that are available in the business-to-business area. And, wireless terminals have long been used to alert service technicians for maintenance and repair.

To date, the preventive maintenance of cars, office equipment, and computer applications is perhaps the most successful wireless application in business-to-business area. The idea is that the products have a subscription to update software components (e.g., virus protection for mobile devices) or to update the microbrowser. How it works is over-the-air configuration.

For example, all software in the product (and many products today have software inside) may be loaded to the product only when the customer takes the product into use. Thus, the number of product variants in the supply chain can be kept low, while the variants offered to the customers are virtually unlimited and can change dynamically in real time.

But to work, over-the-air configuration requires that the supplier can reach the product after the purchase. The implication for value innovations is that not only connecting consumers and supplier businesses, but also connecting products and supplier businesses can create quantum improvements in value. NTT DoCoMo in Japan estimates that within 10 years two-thirds of its "customers" will be devices and not persons. This may very well be a conservative estimate considering the potentials in real-time demand-supply chain management.

■ REAL-TIME DEMAND-SUPPLY CHAIN MANAGEMENT—VALUE CONFIGURATION WITH PRODUCTS AND CUSTOMERS ON THE MOVE

For demand-supply chain management, the interesting issue is: What is the potential for value innovations and efficiency improvements based also on a product's identity and location, instead of just on a person's identity and location? It is here that we will start seeing significant new opportunities that revolutionize the demand-supply chain.

Consider, first, the potential impact of making offers based on a product's identity and location in the grocery supply chain. Wireless product identification can be central to interesting value innovations, starting from when a delivery of packaged consumer goods arrives in a distribution hub until the product is sold to the end consumer. The combined impact of better service and reduced inefficiencies in the grocery supply chain is estimated to yield a 6 to 10 percent increase in total value added.

In the distribution hub, real-time goods receipt and issue makes it possible to speed up the replenishment cycle and reduce buffer inventory. It is a small example of replacing inventory with information, but important considering that goods receipts in warehouses are not always registered immediately and without delay. A one-day variability in the delay before registering the arrival of a delivery translates into one more day of supply needed to run the operation smoothly. Here, the offer of a third-party logistics provider— based on wireless product identification—would be that the product is registered immediately on arrival. This is exactly the same way the business customer was checked in automatically, the moment she stepped into the lobby, in the previous example.

Moving downstream in the supply chain to the supermarket wireless product identification makes real-time inventory possible. Up until now, it has been difficult to monitor what products actually are in stock in a store. Relying on electronic point-of-sale scanning data is inherently unreliable, as even small errors in registering all movements in and out accumulate. And, then there is always the additional issue of shoplifters. But, with wireless identification, it is possible to get a count of all products present—no more need for a traditional inventory management system based on registering receipts and issues. By monitoring category performance and stock-outs more effectively, there is potential to improve sales by an average of 3 percent—eliminating lost sales—in traditional supermarkets. It also allows eliminating checkout personnel, the cost of which is approximately 3 percent of sales, simply by registering the person who leaves the supermarket and the products in her cart.

Combining customization and location when making offerings opens up interesting opportunities for value innovations. The large-scale implementation of the "Capture and Enjoy," "Don't Run Out," and "Plan and Forget" services described in Chapter 5 are all dependent on both the customer profile and the ability of the supplier to identify products in the consumer household. These value innovations also demonstrate how we can further improve customer value (e.g., buying speed and convenience through mobility).

These examples demonstrate the potential of digital services for scaling up service innovations. The required changes for manufacturers and retailers alike will be similar in scope as when manufacturers understood that they do not sell only products but products and related services such as packaging, delivery, and after-market support. Now it's time to realize that manufactures and retailers sell not only products and related services but products and services bundled with various digital relationships.

The essence of the digital relationship for e-grocery is how the e-grocery can become aware of both the customer's demand and the customer's available supply. The basis is access to the customer profile and automatic product identification. But recognizing that the offerings can be made to consumers on the move can uncover new value innovations. Another quantum leap in value for the don't-run-out retail service can be achieved by giving customers the possibility to modify the planned replenishments, check delivery times, and realign the delivery through a mobile device. The value of the plan-and-forget model is also enhanced if the consumer can do the planning anytime, regardless of location, using an electronic Web-based calendar accessed from a mobile device. This combined with the ability to immediately check online the inventory in the household, while tracking all purchased services and goods would let the customer really forget. (The consumer no more needs to think, "I must remember to check if . . . when I come home.")

Wireless product identification makes more robust solutions possible. A traditional VMI solution based on inventory management, registering receipts and issues, is inherently risky. Errors accumulate until a physical count is made. But with wireless identification, a physical count can be done every time the information is needed. Likewise, when a supplier has problems delivering to an intermediary, unfulfilled demand requests accumulate until the supplier cannot accurately judge what the real demand is. The solution is again a combination of product and customer identification—visibility to end user in real time eliminates the accumulation of errors.

Today, a great deal of effort is used in the planning processes trying to guess what has been sold and what will most probably be sold in the future. Think how much easier this all would be if suppliers could really know in real time what was sold every second! With the help of wireless product identification and identification of the end customer, this is possible.

The benefit is particularly large for product introductions. The manufacturer and its partners can, when interaction is digital, directly monitor the success of their marketing activities and use that information for coordinating marketing, production, and distribution. This can significantly improve the quality of planning as collaborating partners can give each other access online about how many people received an offer or saw an ad, how many inquiries that led to, and how many purchases. And, by combining that information with product location information—inventory—accurate responses to promote and fulfill the demand can be made.

Making inventory management mobile has a revolutionizing impact on product recall, safety, and traceabiliy of products in real time. Manufacturing companies know and manage what's happening in material flows within their own premises, but they totally lose the control and visibility of product movements after the product is shipped out. By combining product identification with mobile network technologies and supply chain controlling, we can implement a fully transparent system where all the products on the move are visible and can be "contacted" and managed even after departure. Products can be rerouted to new destinations (even back to the factory in case of quality problems), dedicated to other customers, accurately linked to order status information, and so on. All this means that we are able to replace inventory with information also in the distribution channel.

In the automotive industry where the carmaker often loses visibility of cars as they leave the factory gate, it would be a great advantage to constantly know where, in the distribution net, the products are in real time. For a carmaker that ships overseas, the traceability would allow taking orders and selling off the boat.

With wireless location of products, it is unnecessary to keep a historical trail because the product does not disappear at times from view. The implication is that just as the customer profile can be a unique instance, accessible to everyone authorized, inventory management can be a shared instance that reports product location to everyone in the supply chain.

This also means that the product can have its own identity and interact with the environment. The same way as the customer without ambiguity can indicate preferences through a self-managed profile and interactive input, a product on its way through the supply chain can indicate preferences. We can implement cross-docking from the bottom up, with incoming deliveries instructing the third party to combine the delivery with other deliveries to a certain destination. If a consumer can have a profile in the Internet, why couldn't any product with wireless identification have one, too?

The deliveries indicating preferences for handling is a first step toward shipments engaged in self-service shopping for logistics and transportation from third parties. The other side of the coin is value offering—the VOP. We also need third-party scanning for self-service shoppers (i.e., suppliers focused on the customer demand chain).

Self-service is one of the great value innovations of the twentieth century, but now with both product and person location, it is possible to combine self-service with innovative VOPs. This is the essence of dynamic demand-supply chain management.

A hypothetical example of an innovative new configuration can be set up around the special refrigerators—the reception boxes—for unmanned reception in the e-grocery business. The fact that the consumer does not need to be at home to receive the delivery means that a purchase order or replenishment order can be assembled in the consumer's reception box. Now, there is no need to pick orders in a local distribution center, the OPP can be moved to inventory on wheels, and the inventory on wheels in turn can be automatically replenished when it is easy to locate. Assuming an effective third-party logistics network, the shipments from a manufacturer could simply seek out demand by following a set of simple rules; for example, "Go to where you can fulfill demand with the highest margin." The key is that the shipments have visibility of demand and supply, and supply can proactively position itself to make its value offering just in time.

■ WHAT IS THE TECHNOLOGY TO MAKE IT ALL HAPPEN?

Is this science fiction? No, much of the required technology already exists. It is only the value innovations that have not yet been made.

The basis for real-time demand-supply chain management is that people and products on the move can be always connected to the larger wireless network. Instant connectivity is becoming reality with the introduction of GPRS (General Packet Radio Services), or corresponding packet data standards for networks other than GSM, for mobile phones or handsets. And, with Bluetooth chips (low-cost, low-power radio chips) also falling in price, other devices can be linked to the wireless network.

For handsets, the Wireless Application Protocol (WAP) is important. This is a thin client architecture, which means that the applications are in the network, not in the handset. To understand why this is important, consider how Internet applications work. The browser on users' computers is the thin client, which has no data and no application code. All interesting texts, pictures, and sound that users see on their PC reside on different locations in the Web, over which they can surf with the same browser. And, as there are application service providers on the wired Internet, there are also wireless application service providers for the wireless version.

In the evolution of the Internet, we are about to witness a huge step as it goes mobile. Wireless data transfer rates will improve substantially from today's 9.6 kbps to 2 Mbps and beyond (third-generation broadband mobile networks). For media richness, this means a transition from plain text-based messaging and information browsing into wireless still imaging and ultimately interactive mobile multimedia with online video facilities. The WAP microbrowser gives access to the Internet from a mobile handset.

The projection for the number of Internet users in 2003 previously was around 500 million users, but with mobile access this projection must be adjusted substantially upward. The mobile Internet service i-Mode, which was launched in 1999 in Japan, has been growing at a rate of 450,000 new users per month. This quickly made Do-Co-Mo, the local mobile network operator, the largest Internet provider in Japan with millions of users.

The number of mobile phone subscribers is expected to reach 1 billion during 2003 and to surpass fixed lines. At the same time, Nokia estimates that over 500 million subscribers will have access to the Internet from their handsets by the end of 2003 meaning that by that time there are more handsets than PCs connected to the Internet. According to Forrester Research, half of those users will be in Western Europe and another large portion in Japan. The U.S. lead in (fixed) Internet may prove temporary.

In addition to access to the Internet, location is critical. Locating people and devices equipped with mobile phones is not a problem. Already some mobile networks can physically locate the user at any particular moment. By the year 2002, most mobile networks in the world will be able to position the subscriber within a range of 150 meters with GPS (global positioning system), even a range of a few meters is possible.

Secure mechanisms for authentication, authorization, and encryption—which provide the foundation for secure monetary transactions over the Web—are continuously improved using both the WAP (Wireless Application Protocol) and the SIM (Subscriber Identification Module) Application Toolkit as the basis. Nokia, Motorola, and Ericsson have together standardized WAP for mobile Internet browsing. The improved security also makes it possible to introduce mobility in the corporate systems environment. The corporate intranet, extranet, and ERP applications are becoming wireless with the help of the emerging wireless local area network (WLAN) offerings.

A technology called Bluetooth—a low-cost, low-power radio chip—enables an unlimited number of various devices like computers, computer peripherals, mobile phones, and other electronic devices to exchange information, synchronize data, or transfer within a radius of about 10 meters (about 33 feet). However, Bluetooth is not cheap enough to attach a chip on every consumer product. For locating products and items, Radio Frequency Identification (RFID) is currently the most efficient alternative. This technology was originally developed for automatic identification and data capture in warehouses and distribution centers where hardwiring was not possible, or real-time updating was critical.

The technology has developed quickly, and today new application areas can be found both in retailing and in electronic commerce. It works by attaching a sticker with an antenna, or printing an antenna with magnetic ink on the product, which identifies the product. Then a signal is sent out from a handheld reading device or mounted unit. The product answers the call with the identity that was programmed into the sticker or printed with the magnetic ink.

No power is needed on the product side as the sticker or ink uses the energy in the radio signal to respond. The effective range in 1999 to detect sixty units was about one meter and the price for a sticker less than 20 cents.

The reading device can then be connected to a wireless local area network inside the warehouse, distribution center, shop, or office—the same way mobile phones are in a city. These technologies provide a dramatic improvement over current bar code based identification and allow us to automatically identify, locate, and constantly follow basically any kind of products anywhere.

In the end, it is always the customer's choice that suppliers heed. The implication is that self-managed profiles and requests for offers are likely to be the basis for collaboration. Suppliers that are not prepared to pay attention to the customer demand chain, as the customer presents it, will have a hard time getting any customer attention. Similarly, logistics service providers and component suppliers that cannot make location-based offers (e.g., inventory visibility and cross-docking) may have a hard time winning business. In the mobile demand-supply chain, successful application architectures, built for scaling up value innovations, need to be built up around the unique identities and profiles of both customer and products. The key words for IT applications are self-service by the customer and the ability to support innovative new VOPs.

A value offering and demand chain based on profile, product ID, and location all imply a distributed systems architecture, or a value net of application services. Already, the e-business marketplace has broken down the traditional barriers between industries (e.g., vertical portals). It is no longer easy to distinguish between competitors and partners, and many times the same companies or network of companies are both competitors and partners. As the extended enterprise is being built around end-customer needs and real-time inventory management, there will be new innovative ways to combine demand and supply so that different players in the value net sometimes create demand, sometimes realize supply, and quickly switch roles.

As business-to-business relationships evolve toward a value net of competing and complementing services, we will also see concrete changes in current business-to-business Web sites.

The first phase is the well-known customized vendor pages (see Figure 10.1) set up by single companies like Dell. These are already getting competition from new, less vendor-specific solutions.

In the second phase, new competing solutions are driven by a number of different companies. They are trying to develop a marketplace where customers and vendors can meet by creating standard seller and buyer interfaces and translating from proprietary interface to standard interface. Companies such as Ariba, Commerce One, and Harbinger are only a few in a fragmented applications service business. Different kinds of e-market business models are evolving. Two of the

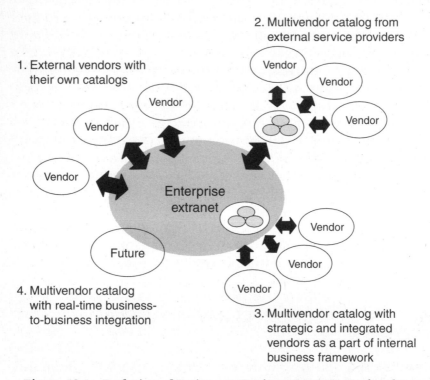

Figure 10.1   Evolution of Business-to-Business Internet Marketplace

most predominant are aggregators and trading exchanges trying to organize vertical markets and making money by domain knowledge, and auctioneers optimizing pricing inefficiencies and making money by cost savings for the buyers.

A third approach is the extranet solution many large companies are opting for. It is centered around an internal e-business engine supplied, for example, by mySAP or Oracle. Anyone that wants to do business with these companies has to adapt its information and tools to fit in that standard extranet solution. Since most customer companies refuse to enter their orders twice (i.e., first in their own ordering system and then in the customized vendor-specific Web page), this means that as more and more business interactions are done over the Internet, the pioneering vendor-specific catalogs will be integrated with their customers' internal e-business engines.

The fourth, and most advanced model is yet to be seen, live. It combines several extranet solutions and includes collaborative planning; shared inventory management, product location, and product data management; automatic payment; and other collaborative business processes. However, industries that realize the full range of value innovation opportunities in the demand-supply chain may move surprisingly fast in that direction. If the e-grocery model succeeds, the grocery supply chain has a good chance of being in the vanguard.

The evolution of the Internet marketplace from point-to-point relationships into integrated demand-supply chains will be based on tools and capabilities linking demand and supply: real-time event information, customer profiles and personalization, automatic ordering and inventory replenishments, product configuration and identification, electronic payment as well as content management. All of these are already in place, or on the way.

■ WHAT DO COMPANIES HAVE TO KEEP IN MIND NOW?

The first thing to keep in mind is that companies with an understanding of the demand-supply chain have unparalleled value innovation opportunities as the Internet goes mobile and reaches not only people and devices, but all types of products.

This is because several reinforcing positive feedback loops are contributing to the development of mobile demand-supply chain management. In the grocery supply chain, wireless identification of product and location makes the distribution and inventory management in distribution centers more efficient. But, it is also starting to affect the way traditional supermarkets can be run. Real-time inventory management makes automatic replenishment solutions more robust and also optimizes categories to minimize lost sales on the store level. Wireless product location also is key for value innovations such as don't run out that make the whole concept attractive to the consumer. And, demand transparency helps move the OPP backward, closer to the producer for customized products, as well as forward, closer to the consumer commodities with a stable demand.

The second thing to keep in mind is that the VOP/OPP configuration can be personalized and local. Here, execution is key. Companies that can develop scalable services and build a customer base by collaborating with other players in their value net may eventually spin off their application, or parts of it, as a new wireless applications service businesses. It is not only telecom operators that will be able to play this game. Real-time inventory visibility of the supply chain is a service that both producers and retailers might want to subscribe to, and that third-party logistics service providers could supply by collaborating. Wireless local area network services for a chain of supermarkets can provide grocery manufacturers with real-time visibility on category performance. And, wireless inventory management services for households can give manufacturers real-time aggregate visibility of consumption.

Finally, managing differentiation and integration is critical for scaling offerings to many parties. The key to integration is a self-service logic. Customer companies need to open up their demand chains so that suppliers can reach customers with new innovative order-less value offerings, but without the customer having to change processes. On the other hand, supplier companies need to maintain a selection of different value offering points, but strive for a standardization of the offering to specific points.

Wireless applications are starting to wipe out the boundaries between the virtual and real world. It is possible to link the physical flow of goods for the supply chain directly into information systems (e.g., inventory management databases are replaced by wireless tracking), and the customer or consumer in the demand chain is directly linked to the supplier business through personal profile and location. With mobile commerce, the digital relationship can be the cornerstone for both communicating demand and executing fulfillment.

The challenge is connecting demand and supply seamlessly but efficiently, without ordering and tedious routines, while retaining the customer's freedom to choose partners. In this book, we have given you a new tool for the task: the demand-supply chain, with examples for configuring it to achieve both value innovations and efficiency improvements. Now it is your turn.

Index